Flowers in the Wild

Marjorie & Desmond Parish

FLOWERS IN THE WILD

Lord, to you we bring our treasure,
Wealth of mind & hand & heart,
Fruit of toil & joy & leisure,
Nature's world & craftsman's art.
Ackn. H. C. P. Gaunt

BLANDFORD PRESS
POOLE · DORSET

First published in the U.K. 1983 by Blandford Press,
Link House, West Street, Poole, Dorset, BH15 1LL

Copyright © 1983 Blandford Books Ltd

Distributed in the United States by
Sterling Publishing Co., Inc.,
2 Park Avenue, New York N.Y. 10016

British Library Cataloguing in Publication Data

Parish, Marjorie
    Flowers in the wild.
    1. Botany
    I. Title   II. Parish, Desmond
    581   Q445.2

ISBN 0 7137 1178 7

Typeset by August Filmsetting, Warrington,
Cheshire
Printed in Singapore by Toppan Printing Co (s) Ltd.

Contents

Acknowledgements

To all those friendly people—and there are many—who have helped us on our botanical-photographic way, in whatever country or capacity, and whatever nationality. We have enjoyed your company and appreciated your practical assistance, interest and encouragement—in lecture halls, at our photographic exhibitions and all the way from beaches to mountains. With this book, we say thank you, with our hope that its pages will revive for you your own personal and joyous experiences.   God bless you all!

Marjorie & Desmond Parish
Wimborne Minster, 1983

Introduction

'Consider the lilies of the field, how they grow'

The distribution of plants and their relationships one with another are amongst the most fascinating aspects of botanical exploration and study. From the confines of a small bog or wood to worldwide intercontinental colonies, one wonders why some plants grow here and not there, or why one colony differs from another on similar ground. Sometimes the answer may be simple and fairly obvious—soil composition, shelter from, or exposure to, prevailing winds—sometimes the puzzle seems unanswerable. It is partly because of this fascination that we have chosen to base our book on ecological habitats rather than scientific classification, national boundaries or colour, and also because botanical excursions are usually, and most easily, undertaken to a specific plant community, whose members grow together because the conditions of that community suit them. So we lead from one natural group to another, with time to absorb the joys and interest of each in turn, to notice the plants' responses and adaptations to varying conditions and sudden changes, and even to note similarities between those of distant and differing terrain, latitude and altitude.

We start our journey at sea level and travel by varying routes and diversions to the alpine snowline at a height of some 3200m, where we shall find we have come full circle—because the bleak conditions of the mountains make similar demands on their plants as do those of the windswept coast.

Northern Coast

This coast is part of Europe's greatest heritage. Many plants growing there are never seen elsewhere and have become adapted to conditions peculiar to land near the sea, including exposure to strong salt-laden winds, saline mud, shifting sand, soil erosion and even periodic inundation at high tide. Yet these plants survive—indeed, even thrive—in such difficult places!

Some of them, especially those of salt marshes, are termed *halophytes* because they can tolerate the high salt content of the available water supply and it is interesting to note that occasional small colonies of these halophytic plants are found inland where salt-mining is established.

Salt Marshes
Salt marshes are broad flat expanses characteristic of river estuaries and regularly covered at high tide. To combat the problems posed by the environment, some plants are fleshy and succulent, with tiny insignificant flowers, e.g. Glassworts and Sea-blite; these are the colonisers, the pioneers which settle in the soft mud nearest low water and so endure the longest periods of tidal inundation. Aided by the seaweeds and the strong *Spartina* grasses, they gradually bind the mud into a sufficiently firm base for others to join them: the colourful Asters and Sea-lavenders, silvery *Artemesia* and grey-green Purslane, whose leaves are covered by short hairs to prevent excessive loss of water.

The higher reaches are often dominated by marsh grasses; they are broken by gullies and salt pans filled at high tide, and fringed with white Scurvygrass and pink Sea-milkwort. The final product of the wild plants' colonisation of the open mud may be excellent grazing turf for farm animals.

Sand Dunes
The problems facing sand-dune plants differ from those of salt-marsh plants in that their soil base is surface dry and they are subject to partial or even complete burial by wind-blown sand. A few shoreline plants may occasionally suffer from tidal inundation. Roots and creeping stems are strong for firm anchorage; this is especially noticeable in Marram, which grows only on shifting sand. Long-term results of Marram's tenacity is obvious in older dunes, where long ridges of hummocky sand run parallel with the shoreline and each other, becoming progressively higher and more thickly covered with mixed vegetation as they 'move' inland.

A wonderful display of plants colonises these dunes, from the scattered foreshore beauties of Sea-holly, Sea Bindweed and Sea Rocket to a rich sward of mat-forming plants of sandy soil generally, e.g. Thyme, Hawkweeds,

Clovers. A glorious picture is provided where hollows are broken by the formation of *slacks*—shallow, freshwater pools—surrounded by moist ground enriched by the lime content of crushed seashells. Here abound in quantity such delightful plants as Grass-of-Parnassus, Marsh Helleborine, Round-leaved Wintergreen, and assorted pinkish red Marsh-orchids, normally associated with inland marshes and often in a silvery-grey-green background of Creeping Willow. Where the inner dune sand is less rich, Heather and allied plants take over with their late summer carpets of royal purple. In all these aspects, and more, coastal dunes make fascinating botanising terrain!

Shingle Beaches
The most inhospitable coastal terrain is shingle, banks of sea-flung pebbles whose seaward slopes are almost devoid of vegetation, although the top and landward side usually support a scattered pattern of often brilliant flower species, such as the purple Sea Pea, golden Horned-poppies, glaucous Sea-kale and Oysterplant. With them are the lovely matted White Campion and Sea-pinks, which are also common on salt marshes and cliffs. Occasional strays from dry inland areas add greatly to this pattern and may include vivid blue Viper's-bugloss, yellow and white Stonecrops and the sinister Henbane, while the truly maritime, evergreen Shrubby Sea-blite emulates a planted low hedge along the drift-line.

These shingle beaches, spits and bars, many of which are separated from the mainland at one end or in the centre, have been piled up by the combined action of strong prevailing winds and the ebb and flow of the waves, which are constantly depositing, lifting and moving the coarse sand and pebbles. This habitat is therefore rarely stable enough for plant colonisation and those plants which survive do so because their roots are long and tough, their leaves fleshy, leathery or hairy to conserve water and, in some cases, their seeds are dispersed by the sea. At least they do not suffer from overcrowding!

Cliffs & Rocks
Of all maritime flora, that of the cliffs is the most varied and abundant because this terrain is the most stable, giving the coast all its grandeur and magnificence. Dazzling white chalk, cool grey limestone, warm red sandstone, sparkling granite, with local intrusions, support a wonderful plant mixture. Grassy tops and slopes are mainly clothed with inland plants able to withstand the salty atmosphere. With them are found specifically coastal species—ranging from the rare endemic Scottish Primrose to the spring carpets of pale blue Squills and Sea-pink—sheer delight when masses of them flower together! Some cliffs suffer severely from erosion by sea and weather, resulting in mounds of bare earth alternating with sticky hollows where quick-growing species provide temporary small gardens until the next rock fall occurs.

Truly maritime plants cling perilously to sheer rock surfaces, rooting in any fissure they can find. They provide a fascinating link with faraway inland gorges and mountains: the rock habitat is the same but the plant species are different, and all survive due to similar adaptations. On the coast, we find misty purple Sea-lavender, yellow-green Rock Samphire and bright Wild Cabbage, contrasting with the bold hard rock. These plants descend to high-water mark where they grow with Golden Samphire, Danish Scurvygrass, Campions and Sea-spurrey, and also with seaweeds and lichens, whose importance in the chain of life here and elsewhere cannot be underestimated. All are subjected to permanent salt winds and spray and typify so well the tenacious powers of survival of the inhabitants of Europe's remarkable coastline.

Mediterranean

Europe's coastline continues to be remarkable through the narrow Straits of Gibraltar and along the northern shore of the Mediterranean Sea beyond Greece to Turkey, and includes a multiplicity of fascinating islands. Much of the coastal belt is now a mecca for holiday-makers. But despite the long lines of high-rise buildings, which must have covered vast expanses of flowering hillsides, taken as a whole it is still one of the continent's richest areas for wild plants. Northern Europeans will rejoice to see their maritime favourites, such as Sea-holly, Horned-poppy and Thrift; they will rejoice also at the breathtaking quantity, variety and beauty of the cliff and hillside plants, many of which are largely confined to the coastal region of the Mediterranean.

Why is this area so rich in plants? The ice cap which blanketed Northern Europe more than 10 000 years ago devastated the plant life there but never reached the Mediterranean, which became a haven for species which were able to spread south. Another important factor is the climate, which displays no extremes of Arctic cold or tropical heat but, apart from local variations, shows a reasonably predictable pattern of mild winters with rain and hot, mainly dry summers. This climate allows a much greater variety of species than that farther north. The region also supports a high proportion of endemic plants. When this once dry hollow basin was flooded, about 1 million years ago, the highest land remained as islands and peninsulas whose isolated plant colonies developed in ways different from each other, and from those on the mainland. The eastern end, particularly the Balkan Peninsula, is especially rich in endemic plants, but the west also has its share, including *Cyclamen balearicum*.

The vegetation of the immediate hinterland has been greatly modified by man and his grazing animals, not least the voracious goats! The familiar cultivated vineyards, olive-groves and sweet-smelling citrus groves now belong to the Mediterranean scene as much as the wild shrubs and flowers, which explode in spring-time into a brilliant display of colour.

The Mediterranean flora is undoubtedly at its most vivid and prolific best after the cessation of the winter rains, before the ground becomes baked by the summer sun. Even February is not too early in the Eastern Mediterranean and April is still spring-like in the west. Among the earliest plants to flower are those with underground food stores, whether bulbs, corms or rhizomes, and the hillsides are bespangled beautifully with hosts of multicoloured Crocuses, Stars-of-Bethlehem, Tulips, Grape Hyacinths and Irises, as well as many rare species. Then follows the main glorious flush of spring, while summer, the season of drought, brings a host of colourful Thistles, well-armed to withstand water loss but with their own peculiar attraction. Autumn produces a secondary flowering season, less varied than spring, but including such unusual and fascinating species as the large-flowered white Sea-daffodil, *Pancratium maritimum*, on the beaches and tall Sea-squill, *Urginea maritima*.

Behind the littoral area, on ground escaping cultivation or building, there is a zone of vegetation usually called *garigue*—with several local names—characterised by a scattered growth of shrubs averaging less than 1m in height. This zone is often extensive and may reach 500m above sea level. Many of its shrubs are typically evergreen as there is little risk of winter frost damage to the leaves. With thick, glossy surfaces, felted hairs and many a prickle, they are well equipped to face the more pressing problem of summer drought. Although not all shrubs have brilliant flowers, the slopes are frequently dominated by glorious stretches of pink and white *Cistus* blossoms, as well as the gold of innumerable Brooms and the rich purple of Lavenders. Among them hides a great wealth of smaller plants, such as Thyme, Sage, *Cytinus hypocistis*, that gaudy parasite on *Cistus* roots, bright *Onosma* and Orchids bizarre or beautiful. Taller Gladioli and Asphodels thrive in open spaces, as do vivid Anemones and Turban Buttercups. The long days of sunshine also bring out the insects, including handsome butterflies, necessary for pollination so that these enchanting hillsides are not only ablaze with colour and warm with aromatic perfume but alive with the humming of a myriad wings.

As we travel higher and farther inland, the shrubs grow more thickly and taller, sometimes reaching 5m in height. They link the garigue below with the forested land above, although there is no hard and fast line or specific altitude to distinguish them. They all merge gradually one into the other; this intermediate zone is the *maquis*. Many shrubs of the garigue are still here, including *Cistus*, Lavender, Rosemary and Broom, and the resinous *Pistacia lentiscus* and its deciduous relative, *P. terebinthus*, are more in evidence. They are joined by *Erica*, especially *E. arborea*, the prickly twining *Smilax* and climbing Honeysuckles, including *Lonicera implexa*. As in the garigue, Orchids and numerous other herbaceous plants provide exciting ground cover. Small trees make their appearance, one of the most attractive being *Arbutus unedo*, the Strawberry Tree, which brightens the autumn with a mixed covering of round pinkish red fruits and drooping greenish white flowers, an overlapping product of 2 years' growth.

No one type of flora has fixed boundaries and at least a few members of this Mediterranean galaxy, e.g. Asphodels and Tassel Hyacinths, are found along waysides and in fields as far north as Central France. Others, including *Cistus salvifolius* and the Lavenders, reach the sun-baked hills of Provence and the Southern Cevennes; this *Cistus* is also found sparingly and protected in the warm Ticino area of Switzerland.

Fields & Roadsides

If we penetrate inland, especially along the quieter roads and lanes, we shall find a wealth of flowering plants which have no sharply distinctive modifications. They belong to a wide range of plant families and display a great variety of height, colour, form and flowering season to delight us throughout most of the year. These are the flowers of the waysides, hedgerows, fields and meadows, the weeds of arable land and colonisers of waste places in both town and countryside. Many are annuals whose individual life span is short but whose small light seeds are produced in quantity to ensure their succession. Some are insignificantly small but they can quickly colonise bare ground anywhere, enabling larger plants to follow them; therefore they are not to be despised. Like the maritime Glassworts and Marram, they play a vital role in early colonisation.

Land disturbed for road-widening, motorway construction and similar schemes, soon supports plants such as bright yellow crucifers and the brilliant scarlet Poppy, long associated with cornfields but now often becoming scarce there with improved screening of seed. As well as these, there are other spectacular cornfield weeds which have now retreated largely to the waysides, including rich blue Cornflowers, golden Corn Marigold and the now rare carmine Corncockle. Among these, several low-growing plants are worth investigation, not least the lovely little Field Pansy, royal purple Venus's-Looking-Glass and the scarlet and blue forms of Poor-Man's-Weatherglass, as the noon-closing Pimpernel is called.

Before roadside verges became subjected to modern methods of control, by rough machine-cutting and spraying with poisonous herbicides, they were the homes of spring-flowering Celandines, Primroses and Violets in quantity, followed by a gay riot of summer flowers and the Hawkweeds, Scabious and yellow Toadflax of autumn. Fortunately, less frequented lanes can still provide much beauty and here Foxgloves, Mulleins, the creamy foam of umbellifers, peculiar spiky Teasels, hosts of Bellflowers and innumerable other species are still to be seen, although not necessarily all together.

However, plants in general are tough. Whatever mankind does to the land, many species, like the Poppies, will survive, even though it means colonising some other habitat, and many can withstand much of our efforts at tidiness! Prime amongst these are Dandelions, whose golden, perfectly formed inflorescences and intricately planned parachute seed heads are everywhere; so are their small relatives, the common little daisy, *Bellis perennis*, whose white petals are often beautifully tinged pink or red. If these plants were rare, how greatly we would prize them! There are some plants which escape from gardens to flourish by the roadsides amongst native species; one such is Winter Heliotrope, *Petasites fragrans*, whose strong sweet perfume betrays its presence before the pale purple flower spikes are seen.

Hedges, although originally planted by man for his own benefit, are now being destroyed in many areas. Their dense growth of flowering shrubs and trees has brought much beauty to lowland roads, in addition to welcome shelter for many herbaceous plants and a whole cosmos of small animals. Spring begins with the lamb's-tail catkins of Hazel, soon followed by the sharp contrast of Blackthorn's dark twigs and pure white flowers. Massed creamy May blossom precedes the scrambling wild Roses, Honeysuckle and Brambles of summer and their fruits provide the glory of autumn; berries of glaucous blue and glossy black, reds and yellows, the brilliant fire of Spindle's orange and pink, whilst the warm glow of Holly berries remains until the year's end. Some hedgerow shrubs possess special modifications to help them climb over their more sturdy neighbours. So we find the slender but tough twining stems of Honeysuckle, the painful hooks and prickles of Roses and Brambles, the sensitive tendrils of White Bryony and the astonishingly thick-stemmed Traveller's-joy upheld by wiry leaf stalks.

Hedges enclose meadows, now often regularly ploughed and cultivated specifically for hay, thus confining wild flowers to verges and corners. Fortunately, hill and mountain meadows are a wonderful compensation still, offering a rich variety of plants, yet also providing good hay. Visitors to such areas will be astonished and delighted by the display of densely crowded summer species: Bellflowers and their odd-looking spiky relatives, the Rampions, Bistort, Dog-daisies, Crane's-bills and countless others. Water meadows have their own special features, although here the scene may be dominated by one or two species only. Brilliant Marsh-marigolds offset by delicate Cuckooflowers are still widespread; rare and local are the waves of chequered pink Fritillaries, while the Summer Snowflake, *Leucojum aestivum*, stands tall, cool and white by the river's edge. In vivid contrast, Marsh-orchids may scatter hundreds of dark purple or pink spikes amongst the grass from maritime slacks to the high alps.

Nothing in the plant world is static and no spare land lies empty for long as every gardener knows! Waste places soon become green with tiny seedlings competing for a place in the sun and it is of great interest to observe the results of this natural regeneration. What comes first? Where from? Which survive? Whatever the open ground—a cutting or embankment for a new motorway, a demolition site in a town, a mining spoil-heap, a disused quarry, a new tipping of waste material, a crop manured with wool-shoddy, or an area around an airport or dock, with a perpetual international exchange of people and freight—it will soon be colonised by wild plants. Of these so-called weeds, some are ephemeral, others tenacious and long-lasting; some are pests, both native and introduced. Thus, to choose only a few examples, lime tips become colonised by wild Orchids, motorway verges splashed with Primroses, wayside corners blue with Borage, and bomb-sites and town backyards bright with Rosebay Willowherb, Oxford Ragwort and, not least, the ubiquitous Colt's-foot.

Woodlands

Roadside hedges frequently border woodland and it is not surprising that many a plant of shady road verges grows equally well on the other side of the hedge. This is particularly true of those which thrive best in partial shade or which flower in spring-time, when the woodland undergrowth is at its most beautiful. Before the trees burst into leaf, many herbaceous plants take advantage of warm spring sunshine to flower early in the year so that a wilderness of thicket and thorn comes to life when, wearied by winter, we need it most. By using their own food reserves, bulbous plants such as Snowdrops, Daffodils and, a little later, Bluebells are able to produce wonderful and welcome drifts of colour; Wood Anemones achieve the same effect with the aid of creeping underground rhizomes. Primroses, Violets, and delicately flowered Wood Sorrel and Ground-Ivy are equally lovely but more scattered, frequently around tree-bases and in hollow stumps.

These all flower before being overwhelmed by Dog's Mercury, whose spikes of tiny green flowers, large leaves and creeping stems are frequently dominant. Quite a few woodland plants have green flowers, but the others are less frequent and easily overlooked. Fascinating Green Hellebores are confined to lime-based woods and mountain scrub where they are more obvious; peculiar Herb-Paris is well camouflaged, often among Dog's Mercury; but the Solomon's-seals and Baneberry betray their presence with light greenish cream flowers. As spring yields to summer, colourful Early-purple Orchids appear, usually in small groups where soil is moist. With thickening of the overhead leaf canopy, competition amongst the undergrowth becomes fierce. Tall strong Bellflowers and Foxgloves grace clearings and track sides; Foxgloves, especially, spread rapidly after tree-felling operations. Brambles and Honeysuckle scramble almost everywhere, as do smaller purple and yellow Vetches.

A few plants have developed a saprophytic way of life and draw on the decaying leaves around them for their food supply; these include three Orchids: the Bird's-nest, Coralroot and much rarer Ghost Orchid. With their complete lack of green colouring, they all look somewhat eerie in their surroundings of brown fallen leaves. The equally peculiar Toothwort parasitises living tree roots for the same purpose. Wandering through the woods, we cannot miss those other saprophytes—the toadstools or cap fungi—especially during autumn. They are scavengers, occurring in sufficient numbers to keep under control the decaying vegetation which, in woodland conditions of close canopy and high humidity, would eventually block all new growth. Here is yet another example of the vital importance of interaction between the various members of a distinctive community.

Shrubs, those woody plants which seem to fall somewhere between trees and herbs, are naturally characteristic of woodland as well as hedgerows. They are usually much branched from the base and possess no distinctive trunk as does a tree. Low-growing examples include the peculiar tufted Butcher's-Broom and Spurge-Laurel, both evergreen and often missed; the latter's attractive relative, *Daphne mezereum*, displays sweetly scented, pink flowers which have made it a too-popular target for collectors. This also grows in light mountain woods, where we may be fortunate enough to see the alpine form of Traveller's-joy, *Clematis alpina*, whose beautiful, blue-purple flowers bedeck the dark pine branches over which it scrambles. Feathery-flowered *Aruncus* and white *Amelanchier* also favour the mountains where they may be as tall as small trees and are locally abundant.

In mountain woodlands, the trees are not always crowded, more sunlight is available and ground vegetation is frequently varied and colourful. Deciduous and mixed woods especially support a great variety of plants, beginning with the glorious mingling of pale Primroses and blue Anemones (*Hepatica nobilis*) in spring. Summer-time follows with a riotous profusion of Wood Crane's-bill, purple and white, dark blue Columbine (*Aquilegia vulgaris*), yellow Foxgloves and Rampions, and shoulder-high masses of blue Sow-Thistle, pink *Adenostyle* and white, multi-flowered, aconite-leaved Buttercups. It is only very occasionally that we find the outstanding beauties of the Mountain Columbines, *Aquilegia alpina* and *A. pyrenaica*, from the Alps and the Pyrenees respectively, both with ethereally lovely, pale blue flowers, and also golden Lady's-slipper, perhaps the most exotic and most elusive of them all!

When coniferous woods are deliberately planted, especially with trees not indigenous to the country, they rarely show a varied ground flora. But the native coniferous woodlands of the higher mountains and much of Northern Europe to the Arctic region are graced by some of the most exquisite small plants the continent can boast. Here the leaf canopy is always present and the flowering season is short, although in the north, compensation is provided by long hours of daylight.

Mossy, sometimes bouldery, needle-leaf-covered ground is the home of the Wintergreens, whose glossy leaves can survive the winter and give the plants a good start for spring growth. Thus we have the lovely drooping flowers of several *Pyrola* spp. and the charming 1-flowered *Moneses* in wide drifts. The tiny-flowered creamy spikes of May Lily and delicate pink bells of Twinflower are sometimes delightfully abundant, due to the strength of their creeping rooting stems. By the same method, the small Orchid, Creeping Lady's-tresses, occurs in scattered colonies, its pale flower spikes held shyly above a dwarf shrubby surround.

Heaths, Bogs and Wetlands

'What would the world be, once bereft
Of wet and of wildness? Let them be left . . .'

Gerard Manley Hopkins

Wetlands! What a sharp contrast between the small dainty flowers of cool coniferous woodland and the floating rafts of large Water-lilies on open water, where tall, lush, surrounding vegetation is spiked with brown felted Bulrushes! How do these plants live such watery lives? Like their woodland and maritime counterparts, they have developed specific adaptations to ensure their survival in these difficult and peculiar conditions. Most truly aquatic plants, like Water-lilies, are rooted in mud, with strong rhizomes for firm anchorage and continuous vegetative growth. A few, like Frogbit, are free-floating, with fine roots capable of absorbing nutriment from the water. Stems are hollow or spongy and flexible to sway with the current; glossy surfaces of floating leaves discard surplus water and their breathing pores are found on the upper surface only. Submerged leaves are often present and may be finely divided like those of Water-crowfoot, Water-violet and Bladderwort, or flaccid, like Arrowhead and Yellow Water-lily, and thus less easily damaged but able to breathe under water. Water Lobelia's submerged but land-rooted leaves are doubly hollow for strength and those of the extraordinary Water-soldier become sufficiently buoyant at flowering time to enable the whole plant to rise to the surface. Overwintering vegetative buds which fall into the mud ensure a further supply of plants if pollination or seed dispersal—often by water—should fail. In short, these aquatic plants display as intriguing a collection of modifications for a difficult life as any ecological group we might name.

The wet oozy mud bordering lakes and ponds supports a different flora although there is some overlap, e.g. the beautiful Bogbean, Flowering-rush and Yellow Iris seem loth to leave the shallow water. The typical growth of Rushes, Sedges and Reeds can be monotonous when abundant and dominant, but when suitable conditions prevail the variety of colourful plants is greatly increased. Then lake and river banks are enriched with a summer-time profusion of some most handsome plants, including Purple-loosestrife and Yellow Loosestrife—two botanically unrelated plants—creamy foamy Meadowsweet and Angelica, pink Hemp-agrimony and the rosy-flowered Willowherb also known intriguingly as 'Codlins-and-cream'. The pleasing perfume of the purple Mints follows later. Amongst the rarer species are the golden flowers of Greater Spearwort, our largest Buttercup, and the unusual wine-red ones of Marsh Cinquefoil. Many of these possess strong thrusting rhizomes and an unending battle for living space appears to continue among them.

Upland rivers may be bordered by clumps of brilliant Globeflowers, which also appear on wet mountain ledges with purple Crane's-bill and green Lady's-mantles. Here, by bouldery streams and rocky waterfalls, we meet the Saxifrages: the dainty Starry Saxifrage, its relative, St Patrick's-cabbage, and the cascading Yellow Saxifrage whose gold and green is splashed in great glorious bouquets all the way from the Arctic, through Northern Britain, to the Alps and Pyrenees.

In similar situations grow the Butterworts, some of the most fascinating yet bizarre of our wetland treasures—the insect-catchers. Sundews, with their exquisitely formed, shining but deadly tentacles, are usually found in more acid bogs and the Bladderworts imprison and absorb their small prey entirely under water. As these plants grow in soil deficient in certain elements, this is a valuable way of supplementing their nutrient intake.

The dominant plants of acid bogland are the Cottongrasses, *Eriophorum*, whose waving white seed heads are such an attractive feature throughout the summer. Amongst them are rarer beauties, blush-pink Rosemary, creeping threads of tiny-flowered Cranberry, or the feathered gold of Bog Asphodel, which may be dominant locally.

In the hills and northern moorlands, wet peaty stretches of Cloudberry may hide Dwarf Cornel and Lesser Twayblade, whereas drier areas are light green with the deciduous leaves of Bilberry (*Vaccinium myrtillus*), a plant with several local names and many relatives. These are all low shrubs with waxen, pinkish white, drooping flowers and large bluish or red, edible berries. Most have small evergreen leaves, leathery, glossy or hairy beneath, with revolute margins, for loss of water must be carefully controlled. These drier areas are also the home of Gorse, (*Ulex* spp.) and sometimes, entwined and entangled around their branches and those of Heather, the totally parasitic Dodder has developed another method of survival under difficulties.

And so we reach the glory of the true Heather moorland, purple for mile upon mile with the massed flowers of *Calluna vulgaris* stretching into the distant haze of late summer. Flowering before and with it, is its darker purple relative, *Erica cinerea*, while the equally lovely pink *E. tetralix* occurs frequently in somewhat damper areas. Less widespread are other Heaths and, very locally, the ethereally beautiful Marsh Gentian. But still the ground is poor in nutriment, including nitrogen, and the Heathers have developed a partnership with certain fungi by which they receive nitrogen through their roots, while the fungi receive other products in exchange. Thus the partnership benefits both—another remarkable instance of the importance of these apparently insignificant plants within the community. All have their value and their place!

> 'O let them be left, wildness and wet;
> Long live the weeds and the wilderness yet'
>
> *Gerard Manley Hopkins*

Chalk and Limestone

In marked contrast to the deficient soil of bogs and heaths, that of calcareous land carries the most varied flora of all. To walk the open rounded hills of chalk downland and the grassy tops of its breezy cliffs, to scramble across limestone scree and fissured pavement or explore its magnificent gorges reveals an enthralling profusion of plant life. Many of these calcicolous plants will grow on both chalk (which possesses the greater percentage of calcium carbonate) and limestone, but others appear to be restricted to one or the other, possibly due more to climate than rock; chalk land is usually present in districts of lower rainfall. Several plants, such as Bird's-foot-trefoil and Thyme, whose tangy perfume is typically evocative of downland on a warm summer day, thrive in almost any comparatively dry soil.

As we saw in the section on fields generally, much chalk grassland has recently disappeared under the plough, thereby restricting wild flowers largely to steep slopes, old quarries, odd corners and nature reserves. But changes in the use of downland are certainly not new. Through the centuries, it has been a favourite dwelling place of mankind, as evidenced by the relics left behind: standing stones, barrows or graves, earthworks, and old forts whose steep sides have become today's havens for many lovely plants—Clustered Bellflowers, Harebells, Bee Orchids, Gentianellas and tiny Lady's-tresses. The landscape has also been greatly influenced by man's early forest-clearing and the introduction of rabbits and sheep, whose grazing benefited the shorter colourful plants. The more recent near-extermination of rabbits by myxomatosis and the partial change from sheep farming to arable farming have altered the floral picture again. However, if chalk grassland were left untouched, tall grasses would overgrow the shorter species, then shrubs would invade, leading finally to re-afforestation.

Where short chalk grassland still exists, however, so do the flowers. Thyme and Squinancywort complement each other delightfully on low hummocks; golden Horseshoe Vetch abounds, as do the knobbly heads and cucumber-flavoured leaves of Salad Burnet. Foamy-flowered Dropwort, bristly but beautiful blue Viper's-bugloss, Rampions and Rock-roses, and the bluest of all the Milkworts—all are there. Cowslips are not confined to the chalk but are frequently found there on the less dry areas, sometimes providing a glorious foil for the Pasqueflower and Early-purple Orchid.

Chalk is rightly renowned for its comparative abundance of Orchids, from the showy pink-purple spikes of the Pyramidal and Fragrant species to the insignificant greenish Frog and Musk Orchids, and the most delightful little Burnt-tip. The Bee Orchids (*Ophrys* spp.), widespread throughout Europe, are scarce in the British Isles, where their 4 representatives are found on calcareous ground. The frilly-crinolined Lady Orchid (*Orchis purpurea*) grows from open downland to light chalky-based woods, with Butterfly-orchids and several Helleborines.

Limestone, especially the widespread grey Carboniferous type, is a harder, bolder rock than chalk. It is seen at its best in the outstanding and magnificent scenery of the scars and pavement of Northern England, the grand sweep of the Burren hills from sea level in Western Ireland, through the great gorges of Central-Southern France to the awe-inspiring pinnacles of the Italian Dolomites, and stretching to the apparently bleak karst of Yugoslavia.

One of the most peculiar and exciting features of this formation is the flat-topped broken pavement often found above equally exciting sheer cliffs. The fissures, sometimes deep, collect moist humus and soon become filled with ferns and other plants usually associated with woodland, like the widespread Herb-Robert and the rarer Baneberry, whose flowers appear at ground level and so avoid the effects of the almost ever blowing wind and occasional sheep. Plants here need to be long-rooted and of short stature and so those which can sprawl over the stones survive. Carpets of prickly Burnet Roses and tough little Mountain Avens provide a white contrast to the vivid, purple-red Bloody Crane's-bill, golden Rock-roses and brilliant tufts of Spring Adonis. A few stunted trees and shrubs may grow here: Ash, Hazel, Hawthorn or Juniper, often bent horizontally to the force of the prevailing wind. The more stable grassland below the scree is ablaze with colour in summer-time with Bellflowers, Mulleins, Agrimony, Knapweeds, Scabious and countless others, many already recorded on the chalk and elsewhere. Locally, blue sheets of *Aphyllanthes* delight the visitor to the Cevennes and, in scattered colonies in several countries, even the elusive Lady's-slipper (*Cypripedium calceolus*) may be found.

For the agile botanist, rocks and cliff ledges are the less accessible homes of various lovely *Dianthus* species, rich blue, erect, spiked Speedwells, Dark-red Helleborine (*Epipactis atrorubens*) and a host of golden composites.

From this brief account of calcicolous plants and their habitat, it will, we hope, be understood why we have devoted a section to the flora of this one specific type of rock formation. The quantity, quality and variety of species and the terrain itself are so distinctive and yet include members of every other botanical group of our choice. The coast, the Mediterranean, waysides, fields, woods, some wetlands, and mountains all have their share of lime-based soil and its rich flora. The really acid ground of heaths, moors and bogs is the only exception.

Mountains

It is but a step, theoretically, from the grandeur of limestone cliffs and gorges to the broader and higher spectrum of the mountains. From Arctic Europe almost to the Mediterranean, and from Western Spain to Russia, they rise in all their varied magnificence above and beyond our previous wanderings, yet they display floral links with them all. Indeed, one of the most fascinating aspects of mountain botanising is that some high-growing plants can be found at much lower altitudes in northern Europe—even occasionally at sea level! We can therefore enjoy such lovely plants as Mountain Avens, Purple and Yellow Saxifrages, and even—although rarely—Spring Gentians down by the sea! Their special modifications fit them for both types of terrain.

As we have seen from the beginning, the plant life of any region is dependent upon several factors: climate, underlying rock and soil, latitude, altitude and local circumstances. In mountain areas, these local features are exceptionally important. Whether a mountainside faces north or south is of great significance; the shelter from drying winds provided by even one shoulder of firm rock can be decisive; the thin layer of organic material lodged in rock fissures—primarily from those small but important lichens—can start a new colony. A local snow avalanche, dislodging tonnes of stones and soil, uproots some plants, but provides fruitful ground for others lower down.

To combat these hazards, alpine plants possess exceptional characteristics of hardihood. The flannel-like coat of Edelweiss, finely beautiful hairs of Spring Anemones, leathery leaves of Rhododendrons, the long roots of scree plants and the quick-flowering of Soldanellas give some idea of the variety and ingenuity of these adaptations. Vegetative methods of reproduction often supplement the normal means, such as the bulbils of Drooping Saxifrage, Orange Lily, Alpine Bistort and some grasses, and the trailing runners of Creeping Avens. Most alpine plants are perennial; summer is too short a time for them to complete their life cycle. There are a few exceptions, notably the incredibly brilliant blue, small, annual *Gentiana nivalis*.

Alpine pastures in spring are unique, partly because the emergence and flowering of plants as the snow melts are unbelievably sudden and rapid. Indeed, the first ones bloom immediately around and through the snow, especially Soldanellas and Crocuses. Opalescent Spring Anemones, pale yellow Oxlips and White Buttercups, especially the Pyrenean Buttercup, follow quickly in such countless thousands that the whole effect is superbly lovely. These early flowering species are able to develop their flower buds beneath the snow or to enclose them in protective bracts and thus reap the benefits of light and space before the great flush of summer vegetation takes over.

But the important terrain for us is that which towers above the pastures and forests: the crags, cliffs and screes, even to the perpetual snow line. So vast is this zone, and so varied in rock and corresponding flora, that we have chosen three specific examples to illustrate and epitomise the whole.

First is a Scottish mountain where, just below the top, at about 1150m, the bold stark cliffs, relieved by sparkling mica schist, are glorious in July with trailing cascades of rosy Moss Campion. This is one of the most widespread and adaptable mountain plants and the moist atmosphere and soil of the north seem to result in a fascinatingly different scale of plant from the usual, tightly-compact cushions of the Alps. The glaucous leafy stems of Roseroot, hang out horizontally, thus ensuring maximum sunlight for themselves and their clustered yellow flowers. Narrow ledges are carpeted with tough prostrate stems and beautifully netted leaves of Reticulate Willow; in contrast, there are the tiny fairy-like plants of Alpine Meadow-rue, and the brilliance of glowing purple Mountain Pansies.

All are backed by Ferns, Clubmosses, Stitchworts, Alpine Lady's-mantle, Saxifrages and more. Most enchanting of all, the compact clusters of azure blue-flowered Alpine Forget-me-nots make this definitely a cliff to remember!

At first, the shelving ground of the 2770m high pass in the French Savoy Alps appears to consist only of stones and snow-filled hollows, surrounded by snow-capped heights, even in July. But there are plants in flower nestling flat amongst the stones in isolated patches about 2–12cm across. Here is Moss Campion again, now so neat with tiny leaves topped by a few flowers and plenty of pink-tipped buds. There are golden spots of Yellow Whitlowgrass, pale lilac *Petrocallis pyrenaica*, isolated delicate flowers of Snowdon Lily and brilliant blue Gentians. Glacier Crowfoot likes places damp from melting snow where its white cups are held proudly erect. Purple Saxifrage was plentiful on our Scottish cliffs but past flowering in July. Here, at much greater altitude, its trailing mats bedeck the stones with rich dark purple flowers, a glorious picture and a wonderful example of plant tenacity!

In the magnificent setting of the snowbound peaks of Eastern Switzerland, some 3000m in altitude, rises another steep dark cliff which, in July, is liberally starred with some of the most vivid alpine plants. Creeping Avens mingles golden flowers with feathery spirals of wine-red seeds, Sticky Primrose droops its rich purple clusters and the lighter purple of Alpine Toadflax is splashed with brilliant orange. Glowing chalices of Glacier Crowfoot vary from white to deep pink and cushions of Alpine Androsace are covered with a pale glistening pink of rare beauty. Amongst all these, the wondrous blue mosaic of King of the Alps (*Eritrichium nanum*) reigns supreme.

We have seen Glacier Crowfoot at 3400m, where its usually glossy leaves were hairy, its flowers still large and glowing. At 4275m on the Swiss Finsteraarhorn, it is Europe's highest recorded flowering plant. At these heights there is more snow than rock, even in July, and the plants live their short but brilliant life cycle in scattered groups amongst the stones. Two things we will ponder before we leave them; first the lichens already mentioned. These are comparatively simple primitive non-flowering plants; they produce quantities of fine spores which settle in tiny cracks amongst the dust from the rock. Here they grow, spread and die and, eventually, their organic remains are sufficient to provide a root-hold for the smallest flowering plants which increase in their turn. So we see the muted design of the varied lichens as background to a host of conspicuously colourful flowers. Lichens are widespread where air is unpolluted, but their association with the flowering plants is perhaps most noticeable on mountain and maritime rocks.

Secondly, from where Glacier Crowfoot grows in the high mountains, we can look down on the glaciers solidly filling the valleys with ice, broken by deep crevasses and huge boulders and lined with steep stony moraines on which scattered plants still grow. High above, rise the permanent snowcaps where there is no habitat for plants, even in summer. All this bleak grandeur gives us a glimpse of what the last ice-cap may have looked like, and the way in which the wonderful complexity of Europe's plant world has developed.

> 'Tis distance lends enchantment to the view,
> And robes the mountain in its azure hue.'

Thomas Campbell

Colour Plates & Descriptions

Abbreviations and Nomenclature used in Plant Descriptions

A = annual; B = biennial; P = perennial
Numbers indicate:
  flowering months e.g. 6–8 = June to August
  length of flowering stem e.g. 10–60cm
Scientific names follow Tutin *et al.* (1976) *Flora Europaea* Volumes 1–5
English names follow Dony, Rob & Perring (1980) *English Names of Wild Flowers* 2nd ed.

Sea Wormwood *Artemisia maritima* COMPOSITAE
P. 8–9. 15–40cm. Maritime. Chiefly N.W.
Sometimes the high drier levels of salt marshes assume a soft silvery grey appearance, due to the dominating presence locally of Sea Wormwood. Erect branched stems and delicately lobed leaves are thickly covered with fine hairs. Small reddish yellow flowers grow in loose clusters and the plants are strongly aromatic. Other members of this genus, notably *A. absinthium* and the alpine *A. genipi*, are sources of valuable medicinal preparations and liqueurs. The name 'Wormwood' is indicative of its use as a remedy for intestinal worms.

Annual Sea-blite *Suaeda maritima* CHENOPODIACEAE
A. 8–10. 7–30cm. Maritime. Widespread. Common.
This typical salt marsh plant is a true halophyte. Found frequently below high-water level, it assists the Glasswort in mud-binding and colonisation. Its succulent erect stems are much branched, the branches thickly clothed with thin, pointed leaves, in the axils of which appear tiny green flowers. In autumn, its overall shade of grey-green changes to warm purple-red, colouring the marsh after its main flowering season is over.

Marsh-mallow *Althaea officinalis* MALVACEAE
P. 6–9. 1–2m. Sub-maritime. Widespread. Brackish water.
This tall, lovely plant is completely different from others of saline areas. Locally common on upper levels of marshes and by roadside ditches near the sea, its large, pale pink flowers rise above surrounding vegetation. Stems and fan-like crinkled leaves are densely covered with hairs which make them beautifully velvet-soft. The flowers grow in the upper leaf axils and possess a central column of united stamens, typical of Malvaceae. The roots yield a mucilage used in treating coughs and in confectionery.

Sea Aster *Aster tripolium* COMPOSITAE
P. 8–10. 10–100cm. Most European coasts. Common.
Resembling and related to our cultivated Michaelmas Daisy, Sea Aster is found in most maritime salt marshes in large numbers and, occasionally, inland in saline mud. Although variable in height, the plants are often tall, with branching stems and long, rather narrow, leaves, all grey-green and fleshy. Each flower head usually consists of a golden centre of perfect tubular florets encircled by purple ray florets, but a rayless variety occurs locally and less frequently. After flowering, multitudes of feathery seeds, like little parachutes, are dispersed by the strong coastal winds.

Common Sea-lavender *Limonium vulgare* PLUMBAGINACEAE
P. 7–10. 8–40cm. W. and S. coasts.
Sea-lavenders rank amongst the loveliest maritime plants and *L. vulgare* is the most widespread of several species. Large greyish leaves are radical, up to 10cm long, surrounding the much-branched stiff stems. Though small individually, the flowers are so numerous, in dense 1-sided spikes, that in late summer the grey-green marsh may be transformed into a glorious purple carpet. These plants have no perfume and are not related to the true Lavenders of the genus *Lavandula*.

Glasswort *Salicornia europaea* CHENOPODIACEAE
A. 8–9. To 30cm. Coasts of N.W. Europe.
The succulent Glasswort is often the first coloniser of salt marshes where it helps to bind the soft tidal mud into firm ground. Often persisting at higher levels amongst other vegetation, it is distinguished by cylindrical jointed stems with tiny inconspicuous leaves and flowers. This plant makes a tasty pickle and was once burnt to provide soda for glass-making, hence its English name.

Sea Stock *Matthiola sinuata* CRUCIFERAE
B.5–9. 30–60cm. S. and W. coasts.
This makes a richly colourful picture on windblown dunes and cliffs, with masses of large, lilac-purple, cruciform flowers, especially fragrant in the evening. These grow in loose racemes above tough, hairy stems bearing numerous sinuate leaves, densely glandular-hairy and greyish green. Perfect, ground-hugging leaf rosettes show promise of next year's flowering and are firmly anchored by a strong tap root.

Common Evening-primrose *Oenothera biennis* ONAGRACEAE
B.6 6–9. 50–100cm. Widely naturalised.
This handsome plant, of North American origin, now brightens disturbed or waste land in Europe, including coastal dunes, with tall erect spikes of large clear yellow flowers, somewhat floppy and crinkled. These open afresh each day, usually rather late, and fragrant to attract night-flying moths, then fade the following day. Later, long pink-shaded capsules develop on the still leafy robust stems.

Prickly Saltwort *Salsola kali* CHENOPODIACEAE
A.7–9. To 60cm. Coastal sand, occasionally inland.
On loose sand of seaward dunes, Prickly Saltwort lies often half-buried. Mainly prostrate, its spreading branched stems are stiff and ridged and each short succulent leaf ends in a sharp spine. It is thus admirably adapted to conserve water—a true xerophyte. Like Glasswort (p. 18), it can be burnt to supply soda. The small, green, inconspicuous flowers are followed by hard, rounded fruits.

Sea Spurge *Euphorbia paralias* EUPHORBIACEAE
P.7–10. 20–40cm. Maritime, W. and S. Europe.
Widespread and locally common on coastal sand, the strong erect stems of Sea Spurge carry crowded whorls of fleshy oval leaves. Flowering and sterile stems are produced, which exude a milky fluid when broken. The flowers exhibit the peculiar structure common to all spurges, i.e. they have no sepals or petals, and are tiny, yellow-green and surrounded by showy green bracts. The plants sometimes assume a beautiful orange-red colour in autumn.

Sea Beet *Beta vulgaris* ssp. *maritima* CHENOPODIACEAE
P or B.7–9. 60cm. Most European coasts, except far N.
Sea Beet is common and widespread on shingle, coarse sand and the lowest cliff zone within reach of spray. The large loosely spreading plants have strong, thick roots, somewhat crinkled, glossy leaves and small green flowers, borne in long-stalked clusters. The young leaves are edible when cooked like Spinach. These plants are related to cultivated varieties of beet, including Sugar Beet.

Sea Sandwort *Honkenya peploides* CARYOPHYLLACEAE
P.5–8. 5–25cm. Temperate and Arctic coasts. Widespread.
Common along the drift-line of sandy beaches, sometimes on mobile shingle, Sea Sandwort is a creeping plant with long roots and shining, bright green leaves, clustered thickly along succulent branched stems. The plants help to stabilise the early fore-dunes, sometimes with Sea Couch Grass, and can withstand short periods of tidal immersion. White flowers, with 5 spreading petals, grow in the leaf axils.

Sea-buckthorn *Hippophae rhamnoides* ELAEAGNACEAE
P.Fl. 3–4. Frt.9 onwards. 1–3m. European coasts, except S.E.
Dense thickets of this prickly shrub sometimes cover large areas of stable dunes, across which masses of tawny orange fruits throw a brilliant autumnal cloak. The plants are dioecious, with tiny green flowers passing almost unnoticed in spring, before the silvery grey leaves emerge to cover the woody twigs and branches. Native, but also planted deliberately to stabilise loose sand.

Early Marsh-orchid *Dactylorhiza incarnata* ORCHIDACEAE
P.5–7. 15–50cm. Most of Europe. Widespread.
The genus *Dactylorhiza* contains an assortment of handsome marsh orchids difficult to distinguish. This variable species blooms earlier than its relatives in alkaline marsh land, including sand-dune slacks. The plants are yellow-green with broad, unspotted leaves, hooded at the apex, and dense spikes of usually pink flowers with lips reflexed at the sides and patterned with red spots and loops. The typical dune plant (ssp. *coccinea*) is short with dark red flowers.

Dune Helleborine *Epipactis dunensis* ORCHIDACEAE
P.6–7. 20–40cm. British Isles. Endemic.
This rare plant is recorded only from a few sand-dune areas in Britain, where it grows either in moist hollows or at the edge of pine plantations, where it is usually taller. Similar to the widespread larger *E. helleborine*, its leaves are more yellowish and arranged in 2 rows (not spirally). The small yellowish, sometimes pink-tinged, flowers rarely open fully.

Marram *Ammophila arenaria* GRAMINEAE
P.7–8. To 60cm. W. Europe. Not Arctic. Maritime.
Marram is the first main coloniser of sand dunes everywhere, no matter how windswept. Long, spreading roots hold firm, stems thrust upward again and sand piles up against the plant. Over the years, firm ground is formed, eventually supporting many other species. Flowers are in tight spikes, leaves are narrow, blue-green, ridged and rolled on the underside to reduce water loss.

Sand Pansy *Viola tricolor* ssp. *curtisii* VIOLACEAE
P.4–12. 3–15cm. Europe. Maritime.
Pansies in profusion provide a colourful attraction on many northern sand dunes and cliffs. Purple, mauve, yellow and cream are so intermingled and plants so variable that identification is difficult. The Sand Pansy is low-growing; the stems can grow beneath the sand and sprout new leafy tufts at intervals. The flowers are fairly large and the petals broad, with a long spur. Found very occasionally inland on sand.

Sea Bindweed *Calystegia soldanella* CONVOLVULACEAE
P.5–9. To 60cm. Atlantic and Mediterranean coasts, S. from Denmark.
The pink and white trumpet-like flowers, lying on pure sand amongst shining, rounded, leathery leaves, make a glorious picture. Before unfolding, the furled and crinkled flowers are protected by 2 red-tinged bracts. The smooth, reddish stems are procumbent but possess great strength in pushing through wind-blown sand just above high water mark, thus enabling the plant to survive temporary burial.

Sea-holly *Eryngium maritimum* UMBELLIFERAE
P.7–9. 30–60cm. Most European coasts. Local.
The strange beauty of Sea-holly is matched by its adaptations for life on soft shifting sand. Long roots for stability, stiff ridged stems, thick spiny leaves for water conservation and tightly massed small flowers are all beneficial in this windswept situation. The whole plant is blue-green in spring and summer, flowers deep blue, all drying to sand-coloured in autumn. Occasionally found on shingle.

Sea Rocket *Cakile maritima* CRUCIFERAE
A.6–9. 15–60cm. All coasts except N. Baltic.
Typical of the drift-lines on seaward dunes, the rather straggling Sea Rocket displays numerous white or purple flowers throughout the summer. The narrow leaves are fleshy and glaucous, with margins varying from almost entire to deeply lobed. It can withstand some sand burial and sufficient sand collects around the stems to form the beginnings of small dunes.

Sea-kale *Crambe maritima* CRUCIFERAE
P.5–8. To 75cm. N.W. Spain to Baltic; Black Sea. Maritime.
In spring, Sea-kale spreads purple-tinged, glaucous leaf rosettes over the pebbly shingle. By summer, the plants display crowded inflorescences of 4-petalled white flowers above the long-stalked, dense new leaf growth. Autumn brings 1-seeded pods, like brown marbles, which, when ripe, can float away on the water for several days, thus dispersing the seeds. The young shoots are edible and used to be blanched and cooked like Asparagus.

Henbane *Hyoscyamus niger* SOLANACEAE
A or B.6–9. 30–60cm. Waste ground, often near the sea.
The erect, hairy, malodorous plants of Henbane produce numerous intermingled large leaves and flowers. The former are sticky with pointed lobes and the latter bell-shaped and dull yellow, decorated with purple centres and an intricate network of purple veins. The capsules persist after seed dispersal, surrounded by enlarged 5-pointed calyces. The plants contain hyoscyamine which renders them highly poisonous but provides a narcotic of medicinal value.

Yellow Horned-poppy *Glaucium flavum* PAPAVERACEAE
B.5–9. To 90cm. All European coasts. Locally common.
Throughout the summer, these brilliant golden poppies display a continuous supply of large flowers, 4-petalled, crinkled and soft. They emerge from 2 enclosing sepals which fall after opening and which, like the fleshy, lobed leaves, are blue-green and hairy. The distinguishing features are the curving green seed pods (to 30cm long), which split lengthwise to disperse the seeds over the shingle where the plants usually grow, firmly held by long tap roots.

Sea Campion *Silene maritima* CARYOPHYLLACEAE
P.4–10. 15–20cm. Atlantic Europe. Common.
When the large white blossoms of Sea Campion cascade thickly over cliffs, rocks and shingle in June, the display is one of the finest around the European coasts. Dense mats of stems and leaves are glaucous; 5 petals spread above an inflated calyx and 10 stamens, at first gold with pollen, are dark by contrast later. Although typically maritime and able to withstand much salt spray, this plant also grows occasionally in mountains.

Sea Pea *Lathyrus japonicus* ssp. *maritimus* LEGUMINOSAE
P.7–8. 20–90cm. N. and W. coasts.
Blue-green patches, wide and flat on windswept pebbly shingle, betray the presence of this handsome plant through much of the year, for its procumbent stems are crowded with persistent glaucous leaves. Each leaf consists of about 8 large, strongly netveined leaflets, usually with a short terminal tendril. Vividly purple 'butterfly' flowers appear in summer, followed by green 'pea' pods, about 4cm long, containing up to 8 seeds, which have been eaten in times past when food was scarce. A very long root stock anchors the plant firmly amongst loose shifting stones.

Oysterplant *Mertensia maritima* BORAGINACEAE
P.6–8. To 60cm. N. Europe. Shingle, coast.
Oysterplant is so-called because of the distinctly fishy flavour (reminiscent of oily sardines in our experience) of its large, beautifully glaucous leaves, which grow in 2 rows along the branching creeping stems. Usually found on the shingle foreshore, it is a widespread northern species, reaching its most southerly locality in England. The small dark blue flowers open from pink buds and are clustered attractively in small sprays at the ends of the branches.

Rock Sea-lavender *Limonium binervosum* PLUMBAGINACEAE
P.7–10. 5–20cm. Coasts of S.W. Europe.
This beautiful plant, related to *L. vulgare* (p. 18), grows on spray-washed cliffs above high water and occasionally on stabilised shingle. Each single, stiff and leafless flowering stem arises from a basal rosette of small, spathulate, greyish leaves (2–3cm long) and divides below the middle into several spreading branches, ending in short spikes of mauve-purple flowers. The coloured calyx of all *Limonium* spp. persists through the winter, resembling cultivated species of *Statice*.

Scottish Primrose *Primula scotica* PRIMULACEAE
P.6–9. 2–5cm. N. coast Scotland; Orkney Islands. Endemic.
This exquisite little plant grows only on wind and wave-swept cliffs, usually on damp grassland. It is characterised by a ground-hugging rosette of comparatively large leaves, the undersides of which are very mealy, and by the small compact umbel of vividly carmine flowers. Unusually for a *Primula*, the anthers and stigma are level with each other inside the flower tube when mature.

Tree Lupin *Lupinus arboreus* LEGUMINOSAE
P.6–9. To 3m. British Isles. Introduced, naturalised near the sea.
This unmistakable shrub, introduced to British gardens in 1793 from California, has escaped to flourish on waste ground, especially grassy cliffs and dunes. Typical 'Lupin' spikes of yellow or, occasionally, variegated blossoms rise above masses of long-stalked, palmate leaves. A single flower shows clearly the petal arrangement peculiar to leguminous plants: a wide erect 'standard', 2 side 'wings' and a central horizontal 'keel'.

Meadow Saxifrage *Saxifraga granulata* SAXIFRAGACEAE
P.4–6. To 50cm. N., C. and W. Europe. Widespread.
Throughout much of Europe, the white flowers of this Saxifrage are found along lime-based verges and grassy hillsides. In Britain, at least, it also occurs on cliffs and stable dunes. Variable in height, erect, slender, almost leafless stems arise singly from a loose rosette of stalked, rounded, crenate leaves; the flowers form a lax spreading cluster on the upper side branches.

Wild Cabbage *Brassica oleracea* CRUCIFERAE
B or P.5–8. 1–3m. W. Europe. Maritime.
Cultivated Cabbages originate from this plant of wild and often inaccessible cliff faces, where strong tap roots and robust stems help it to survive erosion, salty winds and spray. Leaves are thick, glaucous and wavy: lower ones with long stalks, upper ones smaller and sessile. Above them arise several spreading, branching clusters of large, yellow, cruciform flowers, followed by long, thin seed pods.

Rock Sea-spurrey *Spergularia rupicola* CARYOPHYLLACEAE
P.6–9. To 20cm. Chiefly W. coasts. Local.
An attractive little plant, Sea-spurrey always occurs on rocks, walls and cliffs within reach of sea spray and salty winds, held firmly by long tough roots. Trailing stems and numerous, narrow, pointed leaves are greyish green and hairy; this distinguishes it from its glossy salt-marsh relatives. Starry flowers, with 5 pinkish lilac petals, are followed by globular seed capsules.

Irish Saxifrage *Saxifraga rosacea* SAXIFRAGACEAE
P.5–7. 5–15cm. N.W. and C. Europe, Ireland, Iceland, Faroes.
This beautiful Saxifrage grows in mountains and by the sea, local but sometimes abundant. Dense clusters of white flowers almost hide the diminutive, finely lobed, often reddish leaves and short delicate stems. It can be confused with the less compact *S. hypnoides* of north-western areas and the widespread alpine *S. bryoides* (p. 130), all known as 'mossy' saxifrages because of their leaf form.

Goldilocks Aster *Aster linosyris* COMPOSITAE
P.8–11. 10–50cm. Mediterranean, N. to England, Sweden.
Similar to the rayless Sea Aster of the salt marshes (p. 18), but found on
cliffs and rocky places, often by the sea, and never fleshy. Linear leaves,
about 2.5cm long, are sessile, green and densely crowded along the full
length of the unbranched stems. Compact terminal clusters of bright
golden flowers consist of about 6 stalked inflorescences, composed of disc
florets only, star-like, with 5 spreading petals.

Reflexed Stonecrop *Sedum reflexum* CRASSULACEAE
P.6–8. 15–30cm. Much of Europe, including sea cliffs.
The Stonecrops are characterised by short succulent leaves, massed
starry flowers and a preference for dry stony situations; *S. reflexum* is no
exception. Its flowering shoots are longer than the separate sterile shoots,
both thickly clothed with evenly spaced deciduous leaves, those on the
flowering stems being slightly reflexed. The short-stalked, brilliant
yellow flowers usually possess 7 sepals and 7 petals.

Burnet Rose *Rosa pimpinellifolia* ROSACEAE
P.5–7. To 1m. Most of Europe, often by the sea.
Low cliffs, limestone pavement and stable dunes are frequently covered
by a spiny thicket of burnet roses whose large white (rarely pale pink)
flowers provide a glorious summer-time picture. The shrub's erect or
arching stems display an exceptionally dense covering of assorted spines
and prickles and the globular shining hips are also unusual for their dark
blackish red colour when ripe.

Carline Thistle *Carlina vulgaris* COMPOSITAE
B.7–9. 10–60cm. Throughout most of Europe.
Carline Thistle is a plant of limestone areas, including sea cliffs and newly
formed sand dunes. Both ground rosette leaves and stem leaves are very
spiny. The pale yellow flower heads grow singly on short side branches,
with a centre of perfect florets encircled by metallic-looking, pointed,
persistent bracts. These are hygroscopic, outspread in dry weather, but
folded over the florets when it is wet.

Sea-pink *Armeria maritima* PLUMBAGINACEAE
P.4–10. 5–30cm. Coasts of W. and N. Europe. Common.
In May, thousands of the beautiful rounded heads of Sea-pink carpet the
salt marsh, shingle and cliffs, while lesser numbers decorate the coast line
from April to October. Growth varies with situation: usually more
luxurious in marshes than on rocks. Long, tough, woody roots keep the
plants in position against tidal immersion, strong winds and even cliff
erosion. It occasionally occurs on mountains.

Spring Squill *Scilla verna* LILIACEAE
P.4–6. 5–15cm. Atlantic Europe. Sub-maritime; cliffs, rocks.
Although locally distributed, Squills often bloom in thousands forming a
misty blue haze on coastal cliff-top grassland. Each underground bulb
produces first a few grass-like leaves and then a single, short, leafless stem,
bearing at the top a cluster of mauve-blue star-like flowers. These are
followed by black globular seeds which are also quite distinctive amongst
the grass.

Sea Plantain *Plantago maritima* PLANTAGINACEAE
P.6–9. To 30cm. Most European coasts. Common.
This widespread plant, chiefly of the higher levels of salt marshes, also on
short cliff turf, is variable in height, with long grass-like leaves, tough and
rounded on one side. The small flowers form long, compact spikes on
slender, leafless stalks. There are no coloured petals but, in summer, the
anthers are bright with yellow pollen, which is scattered by wind.
Occasionally found on saline soil by inland mountain streams.

Wallflower *Cheiranthus cheiri* CRUCIFERAE
P.3–6. 15–90cm. E. Mediterranean; introduced elsewhere.
The sweetly scented Wallflower is best known in gardens, for, in most European countries, those which appear to be wild are naturalised escapes from cultivation. Most frequently found on old walls, it occasionally also occurs on rocks and cliffs, including the coast. The woody-based stems are leafy, with flower clusters above the leaves; each flower has 4 dark purple sepals in contrast to the 4 conspicuous rich yellow petals.

Tree-mallow *Lavatera arborea* MALVACEAE
B.5–8. 60–300cm. Mediterranean and Atlantic coasts.
Tree-mallow is even larger than the related Marsh-mallow (p. 18) but grows on different terrain: dry rocky or grassy places. Shrub-like in habit and much branched, the plants are closely covered with mingled leaves and flowers. The former are stalked, palmately lobed, crinkled and softly hairy, and the large pinkish purple flowers are veined and strongly dark-centred. A prominent epicalyx with 3 segments enlarges later around the ripe seed head.

Common Centaury *Centaurium erythraea* GENTIANACEAE
B.6–9. 10–30cm. Most of Europe. Grassy places, cliffs, dunes.
This, the most widespread member of an attractive genus, varies considerably in size and growth form, according to situation. Usually a single stem arises from a leafy rosette, branched in the upper half and with a few pairs of small, simple, sessile leaves. Each branch ends in a cluster of tubular flowers, whose spreading bright pink petals contrast sharply with the yellow stamens at the centre.

Rock Samphire *Crithmum maritimum* UMBELLIFERAE
P.7–9. To 30cm. W. and S. Coasts. Widespread.
On precarious cliff faces and ledges, and in crannies just above high water, these succulent plants grow, strong in withstanding salt winds and spray. Their leaves are much divided, their flowers small and yellow-green in spreading umbels, and their roots penetrate several feet into rocky crevices. Flowering is followed by an attractive display of hard tawny red fruits; the juicy leaves are good for pickling.

Golden Samphire *Inula crithmoides* COMPOSITAE
P.7–10. 15–30cm. S.W. coasts. Local.
Golden samphire lives usually on cliffs and rocks near high water, more rarely on shingle and salt marshes. The stems are thickly clothed with simple, bright green, succulent leaves, giving a compact tufted appearance. Large, golden flower heads are borne singly, although massed together, on short erect branches, to be followed in autumn by numerous plumed seeds, which are dispersed by coastal winds. The whole plant is firmly anchored by a long, woody root stock.

Danish Scurvygrass *Cochlearia danica* CRUCIFERAE
A.2–9. About 8cm. Endemic W. and N. Europe.
The English name reflects the anti-scorbutic properties of this genus, whose edible leaves are rich in Vitamin C and, in the past, were invaluable to sailors for the prevention of scurvy. The long stalks of the glossy ivy-shaped leaves distinguish this from the larger white-flowered *Cochlearia* spp. of the salt marsh. This plant is small and compact, displaying masses of pale lilac flowers to great advantage on cliffs and rocks.

Tree Spurge *Euphorbia dendroides* EUPHORBIACEAE
P.4–6. To 2m. Mediterranean coast. Rocky places. Not British.

Large Mediterranean Spurge *E. characias* EUPHORBIACEAE
P.3–5. 30–80cm. Mediterranean area. Dry places. Not British.
The strange Spurges are mostly tropical, but some outliers grow in
Europe, especially around the Mediterranean. Their succulent stems,
when cut, exude a poisonous milky juice, which can irritate the skin
severely. Leaves are simple, sessile and numerous. Small greenish
flowers, with no sepals or petals, form compound clusters in the axils of
leaf-like spreading bracts. Each tiny inflorescence contains a few male
flowers, each with 1 stamen, and 1 female flower with a conspicuous
stalked ovary. These are surrounded by a ring of alternating small bracts
and glands; the latter are a guide in distinguishing the species.
E. dendroides is large, forming dense rounded bushes on rocky sea cliffs. It
is pictured with the tall *Agave americana*.
E. characias, also quite tall, is less shrub-like and characterised by the
unusual soft red of the flower glands.

Sea-mallow *Lavatera maritima* MALVACEAE
P.2–5. To 120cm. W. Mediterranean. Local. Not British.
This tall spreading shrub grows sparingly on rocky maritime cliffs. Its
young branches are downy with white hairs, which disappear with age,
but it retains an attractive silver-grey appearance, due to the equally soft
hairiness of the profuse, rounded lobed leaves. In the leaf axils grow
long-stalked flowers, whose pale pink colouring and dark red centres
distinguish this species from the widespread *L. arborea* (p. 30).

Sage *Salvia officinalis* LABIATAE
P.5–7. 20–70cm. Mediterranean. Dry rocky places. Not British.
Sage is one of the best known of all plants; its healing properties were
recognised by Greeks and Romans long ago and its cultivation for use as a
healthful drink and culinary herb is still widespread. The plant's aromatic
perfume fills the air and its attractive, greyish green, crinkled leaves and
whorled violet-blue flowers may be a dominant feature of scrubland and
steep hillsides.

Winged Sea-lavender *Limonium sinuatum* PLUMBAGINACEAE
P.3–9. 20–50cm. Mediterranean. Sandy, rocky places. Not British.
Restricted to warm southern shores, Winged Sea-lavender has distinctive, stiff, winged, hairy stems, rosettes of deeply lobed leaves and
beautiful bicoloured flowers. These, enclosed at the base by toothed
bracts, grow in 1-sided clusters, each with a rich purple calyx surrounding a contrasting pale or white corolla. The persistent calyx has
remarkable colour-keeping qualities. Often grown for flower
arrangement.

Honeysuckle *Lonicera implexa* CAPRIFOLIACEAE
P.4–6. To 2m. Mediterranean and Portugal. Not British.
Among several woody climbing honeysuckles, this species is distinguished by its leathery evergreen leaves, glossy above and glaucous beneath.
They grow in pairs, joined around the stem; the uppermost encircle the
sweet-scented, stalkless flowers. These are in small clusters of about 6;
tubular and 2-lipped, a characteristic of Honeysuckles; they are delicately
shaded from cream to pink.

No English name *Galactites tomentosa* COMPOSITAE
A or B.4–7. To 60cm. Mediterranean, S.W. Europe. Not British.
Many waste places of the Mediterranean region are beautified by this
clustered prickly plant, of unusually delicate appearance for a thistle.
This is partly due to the sharply divided, narrow leaves, cottony beneath,
whose mottled lobes end in long thin spines. The effect is enhanced by the
soft purple colouring of the numerous large flower heads, with feathery
circlets of long-petalled outer florets.

Golden-drop *Onosma echioides* BORAGINACEAE
P.5–6. To 40cm. Mediterranean, Italy to Balkans. Not British.
It is sometimes difficult to distinguish between the *Onosma* species; all are erect, leafy and bristling with stiff hairs and are found usually on stony ground. Leaves are simple and greyish; the tubular flowers are pale yellow or bright golden, drooping in 1-sided racemes. Points to look for are flower colour and the structure of the leaf hairs which, in some species, including this one, are beautifully star-like.

Large Blue Alkanet *Anchusa azurea* BORAGINACEAE
P.5–8. To 120cm. S. and S.C. Europe. Not British.
The intensely brilliant blue flowers of this plant are quite eye-catching, even amongst the profuse brilliance of the Mediterranean wayside flora. Loose, spreading flower clusters terminate the numerous slender branches of the rough hairy plants and the blue is emphasised by a white centre. The simple narrow leaves are greyish with short bristly hairs; the lower ones are stalked, the upper sessile.

No English name *Asteriscus maritimus* COMPOSITAE
P.3–6. To 25cm. Mediterranean. Rocky places. Not British.
A glorious cascade of gold on a steep rocky cliff was our introduction to the marigold-like flowers of this low-growing woody-based shrublet. The plant is tufted and spreading, with numerous spathulate, hairy, deep green leaves. Terminal bright flower heads possess both disc and ray florets above a spread of leafy bracts; the broad tips of the spreading rays are finely but distinctly toothed.

Fringed Rue *Ruta chalepensis* RUTACEAE
P.3–6. To 80cm. Mediterranean. Not British.
R. chalepensis is distinguished from the bitter-tasting Common Rue (*R. graveolens*) by the fine fringe of hairs on the flower petals. Both are bluish green with beautifully divided glandular leaves and numerous greenish yellow 4-petalled flowers in spreading clusters. Flowers have 8 stamens and a prominent green globular ovary, which later turns black. The plant has a characteristic, strong, unpleasant odour.

Hare's-tail *Lagurus ovatus* GRAMINEAE
A.4–7. 5–60cm. Mediterranean, Portugal, Bulgaria.
This beautiful and recognisable grass is widespread and native in the Mediterranean area, but often planted for ornamental use elsewhere. It is usually tufted in growth, with stems and leaves covered with short soft hairs; the upper leaf sheaths are somewhat inflated. The densely packed flower heads are rather egg-shaped, with the widest part below, up to 7cm long and pale silvery green.

Red Goat's-beard *Tragopogon hybridus* COMPOSITAE
A.4–6. 20–60cm. Mediterranean. Waysides. Not British.
The beautiful fruiting heads of Goat's-beards are perfect in their arrangement of parachute-like seeds. All have conspicuous flowers. The common *T. pratensis* is yellow; Salsify (*T. porrifolius*) is pale lilac with edible roots and young shoots; both are British. A rarer type is illustrated, with single heads of dark red florets, encircled by 8 or 9 exceptionally long, pointed bracts.

Borage *Borago officinalis* BORAGINACEAE
A.5–9. 30–60cm. Mediterranean, Portugal. Introduced elsewhere.
The rough bristly appearance of Borage, contrasts sharply with its uniquely brilliant, blue, star-like flowers, drooping in branched clusters. Each flower has a central cone of blackish anthers surrounded by white scales; stems, leaves and sepals are densely hairy. Frequently cultivated for herbal uses, and to attract honey-bees, it readily escapes to flourish locally on waste ground.

Snapdragon *Antirrhinum majus* SCROPHULARIACEAE
P.5–9. 30–80cm. Mediterranean. Naturalised elsewhere.
This large handsome Snapdragon is native on Mediterranean stony places and walls. The plant is leafy and bushy, with long terminal racemes of deep pink flowers. The cylindrical corolla has 2 lips, the lower one with a yellow 'hump', or boss, blocking the entrance to the tube. On this lip, bumble-bees alight, pressing open the corolla to reach the nectar, thus effecting pollination.

Barbary Nut *Gynandriris sisyrinchium* IRIDACEAE
P.2–5. 10–40cm. Mediterranean. Not British.
This lovely Iris, in sufficient numbers, can transform stony ground into a rich blue-purple haze. Variable in height, the 2 grass-like leaves are longer than the stems, which carry 2–4 flowers, rarely open together. These grow in the axils of papery sheathing bracts; the 3 inner petals are narrow and erect; the 3 outer ones are wide, spreading, and centred gold and white.

Dense-flowered Orchid *Neotinea maculata* ORCHIDACEAE
P.3–5. 8–30cm. Mediterranean, Portugal, British Isles.
This small orchid is of great interest because, although its headquarters are in the Mediterranean countries, there are outlying colonies in Ireland and the Isle of Man. Some plants have large spotted leaves and pale pink flowers; others have plain leaves accompanied by white or greenish flowers. All have stout green seed pods. Each tiny flower of the dense spike is delicately beautiful, with veined hood, 3-lobed lip and short spur.

Italian Lords-and-Ladies *Arum italicum* ARACEAE
P.4–5. 20–60cm. Mediterranean, British Isles.
The obvious characteristics of this peculiar genus are the spathe (leaf-like hood) and spadix (erect club). In this species, the spathe is light green with lighter veins but no spots and the spadix is yellow. Hidden within the spathe, tiny flowers, male above, female below, encircle the stalk of the spadix. After an unusual process of insect pollination, a tight spike of poisonous red berries is produced in autumn.

Sage-leaved Rock-rose *Cistus salvifolius* CISTACEAE
P.3–6. To 90cm. Circum-Mediterranean. Not British.

Rock-rose *Cistus incanus* CISTACEAE
P.3–6. To 90cm. E. Mediterranean. Not British.
The pink and white-flowered *Cistus* shrubs provide one of the great glories of the Mediterranean spring. Several species, branched, leafy and aromatic, grow on stony sun-baked slopes from sea-level up into the southern and island mountains. Each flower lives only for a day, but their continuous profuse succession ensures a long flowering season. The leaves, especially of *C. incanus* and *ladaniferus*, yield a sticky gum, ladanum, once used in medical dressings and perfumery.
C. salvifolius has large white flowers with smooth, broad, overlapping petals and reddish sepals. The sage-like leaves are not sticky and scarcely aromatic. It spreads several miles inland.
C. incanus flowers have large, softly crinkled, delicate pink petals; the bright green, reticulate, sticky leaves are highly aromatic.

No English name *Cytinus hypocistis* RAFFLESIACEAE
A.5–6. 8cm. Mediterranean, Portugal. Not British.
This peculiar plant is parasitic on the roots of *Cistus* shrubs and is brilliant red and yellow. The dense flower heads push through the soil beneath the shrubs and their red scales part to reveal yellow, cup-like, 4-petalled flowers. These are unisexual, male (uppermost) and female both in one cluster, with either 8 fused stamens or the pistil visible within them.

Three-Leaved Toadflax *Linaria triphylla* SCROPHULARIACEAE
A.4–6. To 40cm. Mediterranean. Not British.
This attractive Toadflax is named from its rather broad, glaucous leaves, growing in stalkless whorls of 3 along the erect sturdy stem, which terminates in a spike of fairly large, beautifully variegated flowers which are 2-lipped, the upper lip standing almost upright. They shade from yellow to purple, with a prominent orange boss at the throat and a long, downward-pointing, purple spur.

Scalloped Broomrape *Orobanche crenata* OROBANCHACEAE
A.3–6. 20–70cm. Circum-Mediterranean. Not British.
Broomrapes have no chlorophyll and cannot manufacture their own food by photosynthesis. They are parasites, obtaining nutriment from the roots of other plants. The erect stems are usually unbranched with leaves reduced to small scales; there is a dense terminal spike of 2-lipped tubular flowers. *O. crenata*, parasitic on leguminous plants, has wavy-edged white flowers, streaked with violet, and a purple stigma.

Bertoloni's Bee Orchid *Ophrys bertolonii* ORCHIDACEAE
P.3–6. 10–30cm. Mediterranean. Not British.

Early Spider-orchid *Ophrys sphegodes* ORCHIDACEAE
P.4–6. 10–30cm. W.C., S. Europe, Mediterranean, S. England.

Mirror Orchid *Ophrys speculum* ORCHIDACEAE
P.3–4. 6–20cm. Mediterranean, Portugal. Not British.
The genus *Ophrys* is intriguing. Most species are variable in flower form, and hybridisation produces mixed populations, increasing the confusion. They are single-stemmed, erect plants with glossy, unspotted leaves and a loose spike of 2–10 flowers, resembling some form of insect. The flowers conform to the usual orchid pattern of 6 perianth parts (like petals); the largest (lip) hangs downwards and the 5 smaller spread around and above it. The lip forms the 'insect' or 'spider' and is an important distinguishing feature. The usually separate stamens and pistils are replaced by a single structure, the column. These 3 species grow in dry grassy places and maquis.
O. bertolonii has pink- or purple-petalled flowers (rarely green); the long, brownish purple lip has a horizontal, luminous blue patch and a small forward-pointing green appendage at the base.
O. sphegodes flowers have 3 green outer petals and 2 very small, sometimes red-tinged, inner ones. The lip is large, rounded, maroon-brown, marked with a conspicuous blue H or X.
O. speculum displays a blue vertical 'mirror' on the lip, which is densely fringed with brown hairs and has no green appendage. Petals are green, tinged or striped with brown.

Starry Clover *Trifolium stellatum* LEGUMINOSAE
A.4–6. To 25cm. Mediterranean. Naturalised S. England.
The delightful little Starry Clover is named from the flower's unusually beautiful calyces. In each, 5 sepals, united below, separate above into long narrow points, almost hiding the tiny pink flowers. After flowering, these points spread into a silky-haired star, variably coloured red, orange and green. The flowers grow in rounded heads; their stalks and small trifoliate leaves are hairy.

No English name *Centaurea hyalolepis* COMPOSITAE
A.4–9. To 80cm. Mediterranean. Not British.
This thistle-like plant brightens waste ground with compact, bright yellow, globular flower heads, which have no spreading ray florets. Beneath is an unusual spiky star, formed by the involucral bracts, which are prolonged to form long, narrow, sharply pointed spines, spreading horizontally. The leaves are soft and spineless, the lower ones deeply lobed, the upper entire with a short terminal point. Before flowering, the buds resemble spiny bronze balls.

Pink Jerusalem-sage *Phlomis purpurea* LABIATAE
P.4. To 90cm. Mediterranean Spain; Portugal. Not British.

Small Yellow Jerusalem-sage *Phlomis lychnitis* LABIATAE
P.4–7. 20–50cm. S.W. Europe. Not British.
The name 'Sage' for this genus is misleading for, although related to *Salvia* (p. 32) there are differences, e.g. pink, purple or yellow but not blue flowers, and they are not aromatic. Growing in similar stony places, they exhibit typical labiate characters: square stems, paired leaves and leafy whorls of showy 2-lipped flowers, with the upper longer lip arching over the lower one.
P. purpurea has tall herbaceous stems carrying whorls of about 8 softly pink-purple flowers, subtended by long leafy bracts. Below are short-stalked leaves, wrinkled above and very hairy beneath.
P. lychnitis, contrastingly, is woody-based, flaunting bright golden flowers. The stems are less leafy; the lower leaves are tufted, linear, reticulate and grey-green. The flowers' subtending bracts are pointed-oval and the calyces silky-hairy.

French Lavender *Lavandula stoechas* LABIATAE
P.4–6. To 60cm. Mediterranean, Portugal. Not British.
French Lavender bedecks stony hillsides with masses of glorious purple. Old plants are woody at the base. Their upper stems have short side branches, dense with small, narrow, inrolled leaves, felted with hairs. Above these, each stem terminates in a dense spike of tiny, 5-petalled, dark velvety purple flowers, blooming irregularly among the purple-grey subtending bracts. Topmost is a conspicuous plume of 4 purple petal-like bracts, to attract insects for pollination.

Persian Cyclamen *Cyclamen persicum* PRIMULACEAE
P.1–4. 15–20cm. E. Mediterranean. Not British.

No English name *Cyclamen balearicum* PRIMULACEAE
P.4–5. 10cm. Balearic Islands, S. France. Not British.
The delicately beautiful *Cyclamen* flourish from Mediterranean sea level into the mountains in woods and rocky places. From an underground corm grow large rounded or heart-shaped leaves, intricately and variably patterned with silver. Pendant pink or white flowers grow singly on slender stalks, each flower with 5 twisted petals curving sharply backwards over its own short tube. After flowering, the stalk coils around the seed capsule and lowers it to the ground to disperse the seeds.
C. persicum is the fore-runner of the florist's pot-plant. In the wild, its flowers are scented and pink with a rich carmine throat. This is the only species with stalks not coiling after flowering.
C. balearicum has small, scented, white flowers, contrasting with its disproportionately large leaves.

Bindweed *Convolvulus althaeoides* CONVOLVULACEAE
P.3–6. To 90cm. Mediterranean. Dry places. Not British.
The Mallow-leaved Bindweed climbs, scrambles, or intertwines around itself on roadsides and waste ground wherever it can find support for its weak stems. Thus upheld, its short-lived, attractive trumpet-flowers, pink with carmine centres, unfold upward to the sun. The characteristic soft hairy leaves are variously lobed, from the large blunt-toothed lower ones to the fine-fingered leaflets of the upper ones.

Turban Buttercup *Ranunculus asiaticus* RANUNCULACEAE
P.4–5. To 30cm. E. Mediterranean. Not British.
Local in distribution, these brilliant buttercups provide a wonderful display of scarlet, gold, white, pink and pale yellow, separately or variously intermingled. Each large flower has a central dark mass of stamens and carpels; outside are 5 green sepals (the similar Anemones have none). Radical leaves are long-stalked and broadly lobed; stem-leaves are more finely divided with narrow tripartite divisions.

Italian Orchid *Orchis italica* ORCHIDACEAE
P.3–5. 20–60cm. Mediterranean, Portugal. Not British.

Pink Butterfly-orchid *Orchis papilionacea* ORCHIDACEAE
P.3–5. 10–30cm. S. Europe. Not British.

Anatolian Orchid *Orchis anatolica* ORCHIDACEAE
P.3–5. To 25cm. E. Mediterranean. Not British.

Provence Orchid *Orchis provincialis pauciflora* ORCHIDACEAE
P.4–6. 10–20cm. E. and C. Mediterranean. Not British.
These 4 representatives of the genus *Orchis* all display some of its
distinctive features, including single smooth stems bearing terminal
spikes of comparatively small flowers, usually purple or pink, occasionally
white or yellow. Of the 6 perianth parts, the largest is the lip, often
patterned with spots and lines and sometimes a distinguishing character
between species, as is the nectar-holding spur behind each flower. The
remaining 5 parts are usually curved upward into a distinct hood above
the lip. Leaves are glossy, sometimes spotted, the largest at the base and
the smaller ones sheathing the stem.
O. italica is distinguished by its distinctly wavy-edged basal leaves. The
fairly dense flower heads are rounded; the flowers appear delicate though
shaggy because of the long, finely pointed perianth parts and divided lip.
All are pinkish-lilac, striped darker on the hood; the short spur points
downward.
O. papilionacea likes dry grassy ground. Its leaves are long, narrow and
unspotted and the distinctive flowers form a short lax spike. They shade
through wine, purple and pink, with darker stripes on both hood and wide
frilled lip; the spur points downward.
O. anatolica has broad leaves and pale pink, purple or white flowers,
forming a loose spike. 3 perianth parts make the hood while 2 are
outspread. The lip is broad, shallowly lobed and delicately spotted; a long
spur lies almost horizontally or curved upward.
O. provincialis ssp. *pauciflora* has yellow (occasionally pink) flowers, erect
against the stem in a rather narrow spike. The hood is loosely formed; the
lip is brighter yellow with a few red spots, slightly lobed; the long narrow
spur points upward. Leaves are usually unspotted (c.f. *O. p. provincialis*).

Vetch *Vicia lunata* LEGUMINOSAE
P.4. 10–15cm. E. Mediterranean. Not British.
This delightful plant spreads its clustered flowers over rocks, boulders
and dry roadside banks. The leaves, typical of vetches, are pinnate with
about 5 pairs of oval, sharply pointed leaflets and a short terminal tendril.
The flowers are variegated: the broad standard mauve with darker veining
and the pale yellow keel enfolded by 2 golden wings. Crescent-shaped
seed pods give it the name '*lunata*'.

Bermuda Buttercup *Oxalis pre-caprae* OXALIDACEAE
P.2–4. 15–30cm. Mediterranean, W. Europe. Not British.
One of the brightest displays of spring in the Mediterranean area is
provided by one of the worst plant pests, a South African native,
introduced via Bermuda for ornament. It spreads rapidly by producing
bulbils at ground level, which makes eradication difficult. Lemon-yellow
flowers, wide open only in morning and early afternoon sunlight, grow in
long-stalked umbels amid numerous clover-like leaves.

Golden Henbane *Hyoscyamus aureus* SOLANACEAE
P.3–7. 30–60cm. E. Mediterranean. Not British.
All Henbanes are poisonous and have past associations with witchcraft.
This species is exceptionally decorative, with bright golden flowers, deep
purple at the throat. The dense mingling of these and large woolly leaves,
irregularly toothed and lobed, provides an attractive display on old walls
and cliffs. The bell-like corollas are unevenly lobed, the 3 upper lobes
being larger than the 2 lower ones.

Judas Tree *Cercis siliquastrum* LEGUMINOSAE
P.3–5. To 10m. Mediterranean. Not British.
Several unusual trees and shrubs attract the attention of visitors to the Mediterranean. In spring-time, glorious purple-pink blossoms cover the Judas Tree before its leaves appear, growing not only from branches but even from the trunk itself in hanging bunches of Sweet-Pea-like flowers. This is reputedly the tree from which Judas Iscariot hanged himself, since when its flowers always blush with shame.

Lentisc *Pistacia lentiscus* ANACARDIACEAE
P.4–6. 1–3m. Mediterranean, Portugal. Not British.
Amongst the varied shrubs of the maquis, this very useful one is conspicuous in spring, when its twiggy branches are decorated with tight clusters of small flowers. There are no petals; the anthers glow bright dark red against a background of glossy evergreen leaves. The plant is aromatic and, from the bark, resin is collected for several purposes, including medicines, varnish and chewing-gum-like sweetmeats.

Canary Palm *Phoenix canariensis* PALMAE
P.5. 6–8m. Mediterranean. Introduced. Not British.
Brought from the Canary Islands and planted for ornament along Mediterranean promenades, this tree is now a prominent feature. The large spreading terminal tufts of shining sharp-pointed leaves provide welcome shade and fibrous leaf bases cover each stout trunk. The flowers grow in clusters amongst the leaves and the small brown fruits are dry and tasteless, unlike those of the related Date Palm.

Castor-oil Plant *Ricinus communis* EUPHORBIACEAE
A or P.2–12. 1–3m. Mediterranean. Introduced. Not British.
This native of the tropics is both attractive and useful. Robust and fast-growing, it produces large, long-stalked leaves, divided into several unequal lobes with toothed edges. Flowers grow in erect clusters: female ones above, with bluish green spiky ovaries topped by 3 red styles and male flowers below with conspicuous bunches of yellow stamens. Castor oil is obtained from the seeds.

Spanish Broom *Spartium junceum* LEGUMINOSAE
P.5–8. 1–3m. Mediterranean, S.W. Europe. Not British.
When the hillslopes above the sea are clothed and scented with Brooms, what wealth of beauty they provide. Chief among them is *Spartium junceum*, not spiny but with sparsely leaved, stiff branches and large, clear yellow flowers of typical leguminous structure (p. 26). The flowers yield a yellow dye, the stems a fibre for basket-weaving and, in Britain, it is sometimes planted on dunes to enrich the sand with nitrogen.

Strawberry-tree *Arbutus unedo* ERICACEAE
P.10–4. 10m. Mediterranean, S.W. Europe. Ireland.
The evergreen Strawberry Tree is peculiarly attractive in October when the current year's flowers are present together with fruits from the previous year. The clustered flowers are small, urn-shaped and greenish white. The conspicuous strawberry-like fruits are yellow at first, red when ripe, with a rough surface, and not very palatable. Its distribution is interesting: widespread through the Mediterranean, it is locally native north to Ireland, and is often planted elsewhere.

Prickly-pear *Opuntia ficus-indica* CACTACEAE
P.6–7. 3–5m. Mediterranean. Introduced. Not British.
Imported from tropical America, this extraordinary and unmistakable cactus is now widespread throughout the Mediterranean. Instead of normal stems and leaves, large flat green pads branch one from another, with a regular pattern of sharp spines. Attractive yellow flowers grow on the margins of the pads, followed by yellow or red fruits, pulpy and edible. These cacti make good hedges for deterring animals.

Giant Hogweed *Heracleum mantegazzianum* UMBELLIFERAE
P.6–9. To 4m. Caucasus. Introduced and naturalised elsewhere.
Introduced originally for ornament, this plant is now established on waste ground in several European countries, including Britain, where its exceptional size and height always attract attention. Stems are furrowed, red-spotted and hollow; leaves deeply lobed and toothed. The white flowers are displayed in spreading umbels. After fruiting the stems collapse and die; they exude a poisonous substance, damaging to the skin.

White Bryony *Bryonia cretica* ssp. *dioica* CUCURBITACEAE
P.5–9. To 1m. Most of Europe. Hedges, scrub, locally common.
White Bryony is most attractive when threading autumnal hedges with strings of its bright yellow and red (but poisonous) berries. Later, the stems die down, to be replaced by fast-growing new ones in spring, when, with their large palmate leaves, they are pulled upwards by spirally twisted sensitive tendrils, which change direction of coil in the middle. The plant is dioecious with clusters of small green flowers.

Pyramidal Star-of-Bethlehem *Ornithogalum narbonense*
LILIACEAE   P.4–6. 30–60cm. Chiefly Mediterranean.

Spiked Star-of-Bethlehem *O. pyrenaicum* LILIACEAE
P.5–7. 45–90cm. Most of Europe, except N.

Star-of-Bethlehem *O. umbellatum* LILIACEAE
P.4–5. 10–30cm. Most of Europe. Grassy places.
The genus *Ornithogalum* contains several beautiful species, usually with single erect flowering stems, long basal leaves and wide, starry, white flowers, backed by a green stripe on each of the 6 separate petals. They are bulbous plants, preferring stony or grassy sunny places and frequently found on roadsides and waste ground. These 3 species all penetrate northwards; *O. pyrenaicum* and *umbellatum* occur locally in England.
O. narbonense is distinguished by its long spike of numerous, rather small, but brilliantly white flowers, overtopping the linear leaves. The young flower stalks spread outwards but press closer to the stem as the flowers develop, giving an overall pyramidal appearance.
O. pyrenaicum, known in England as Bath Asparagus because of its edible young shoots, has rather small yellow-green flowers with very narrow petals, growing in an elongated spike. The glaucous linear leaves often wither by flowering time.
O. umbellatum differs from both the preceding species in the grouping of its flowers in a flat-topped cluster on stalks of varying lengths. The fairly broad petals are spreading, white and star-like, with a green stripe outside; the grooved leaves possess a white mid rib.

Common Honeysuckle *Lonicera periclymenum* CAPRIFOLIACEAE
P.6–9. To 6m. Most of Europe. Hedgerows, woods. Common.
Honeysuckle is a beautiful hedgerow plant whose wiry stems twine clockwise around the stronger shrubs. Tough and woody, with simple dark bluish-green leaves, its sweet-scented flowers grow in circular terminal clusters. Each long tubular 2-lipped corolla, from which 5 stamens and the style protrude, is shaded with pink, cream and yellow. Tight clusters of bright red poisonous berries follow in autumn.

Shepherd's Cress *Teesdalia nudicaulis* CRUCIFERAE
A.4–6. 8–30cm. Most of Europe. Sandy, gravelly places.
Usually insignificant, and superficially resembling several other small cruciferous plants, Shepherd's Cress has some interesting specific features. From a basal rosette of stalked, deeply lobed leaves arise several slender, almost leafless, stems, the centre one always without leaves—hence 'nudicaulis'. Tiny white flowers grow in terminal clusters on the stems, each flower with 4 petals, 2 distinctly bigger than the others. The stems elongate as the rounded green seed pods develop.

Rosebay Willowherb *Epilobium angustifolium* ONAGRACEAE
P.6–9. 30–120cm. Most of Europe. Clearings, disturbed ground.
The rosy-flowered plants of Rosebay Willowherb, or Fireweed, quickly colonise waste ground, especially after fire damage. Numerous simple leaves grow spirally around each tall unbranched stem, below a terminal raceme of large, 4-petalled flowers. There are 4 narrow purple sepals, 8 white stamens and a protruding style with 4 stigmas. In autumn, long narrow pods split lengthwise to release quantities of silkily plumed seeds.

Common Mallow *Malva sylvestris* MALVACEAE
P.6–9. 30–90cm. All of Europe. Roadside verges, waste ground.
This common relative of the exotic *Hibiscus* is a much-branched straggly plant, very leafy, with numerous large purple flowers in the leaf axils. The 5 separate petals are marked with dark purple; stamens are united around the styles and stigmas, (typical of Malvaceae); the outer epicalyx has 3 separate segments. The leaves are stalked, hairy like the stems and buds, and palmately lobed with crenate margins.

Red Valerian *Centranthus ruber* VALERIANACEAE
P.5–9. 30–60cm. S. Europe. Introduced elsewhere.
Native only in the south, this plant is cultivated for ornament and has spread widely over cliffs and walls. Glossy stems carry several pairs of triangular or broad pointed leaves and large attractive clusters of small flowers, usually deep red, sometimes white, each with a long narrow 5-lobed corolla-tube, only 1 stamen and a tiny basal spur. These last 2 points distinguish *Centranthus* from *Valeriana*.

Thyme *Thymus drucei* LABIATAE
P.6–8. 8–15cm. All Europe. Dry grass, rocks, dunes, mountains.
This charming plant scents the air with its aromatic perfume on warm summer days. Long-rooted and low-growing, its thread-like creeping stems form dense mats, covered with tiny, oval, paired leaves and terminal rounded heads of small, lilac-purple, 2-lipped flowers. Widespread, it often covers large areas with massed colour. Amongst its several relatives is the culinary herb, *Thymus vulgaris* (p. 106).

Maiden Pink *Dianthus deltoides* CARYOPHYLLACEAE
P.6–9. 15–45cm. All Europe, except Ireland. Dry fields, woods.
This lovely compact plant nestles amongst grass, where it forms rounded cushions up to 20cm across. Tufts of short, non-flowering stems and small, paired, glaucous leaves are almost hidden by massed, small, scentless flowers of deep rich pink, with centres beautifully spotted and ringed. An outer epicalyx of 2–4 scales is about half the length of the long tubular calyx, above which radiate 5 petals with finely toothed margins.

Corncockle *Agrostemma githago* CARYOPHYLLACEAE
A.4–8. 30–100cm. Mediterranean. Native; introduced elsewhere.
This vividly beautiful plant has poisonous black seeds and, being a cornfield weed, any mixing of the seed with the corn can seriously affect the flour. Good screening has drastically reduced its numbers and it is now quite rare. It grows as tall as corn, with solitary large carmine flowers, lightly blue-spotted inside, with 5 spreading sepals, unusually long, pointed and hairy.

Selfheal *Prunella vulgaris* LABIATAE
P.6–9. 5–30cm. All Europe. Grassy places. Common.
From Selfheal's creeping stems grow roots and erect leafy flowering shoots, all slightly hairy. The dark green leaves are paired, entire, broadest near the base. Bilabiate flowers are dark purple-blue, usually 6 in each terminal, compact, flat-topped inflorescence, amid small leaf-like purplish green bracts. It has a good reputation as a healer of wounds. Do not confuse with Bugle, *Ajuga reptans*.

Woad *Isatis tinctoria* CRUCIFERAE
B.5–8. 90–120cm. Throughout Europe. Often naturalised; rarely in England.
Waving yellow panicles of the massed small flowers of Woad brighten roadside verges and waste grassland, although locally, especially where it has escaped from past cultivation. The plant was once valued for the blue dye obtained from its glossy blue-green leaves and used centuries ago as war paint and, later, as a dye for cloth. The seed pods are quite distinctive, green turning brown and hanging like bunches of small keys.

Cypress Spurge *Euphorbia cyparissias* EUPHORBIACEAE
P.5–6. 15–40cm. Much of Europe. Grassland.
This most attractive plant resembles a small coniferous tree in its bushy, leafy appearance. Numerous narrow sessile leaves clothe the erect branched stems below the umbels of small greenish yellow flowers, which are held above the paired bracts. Each flower gland has 2 short curved horns. The plant, especially leaves and bracts, frequently displays beautiful shades of yellow and crimson.

White Mullein *Verbascum lychnitis* SCROPHULARIACEAE
B.50–150cm. 6–9. Most of Europe. Dry waste ground.

Hoary Mullein *Verbascum pulverulentum* SCROPHULARIACEAE
B.50–120cm. 6–9. C. and S. Europe. Dry waste ground.
The several species of *Verbascum* may be difficult to distinguish, partly because of hybridisation; they are always hairy, with large basal leaf rosettes and alternate stem leaves. On tall, usually branched stems grow small clusters of showy yellow (occasionally white) flowers. Above a very short tube, 5 rounded petals alternate with 5 stamens; some or all of the filaments are beautifully clothed with white or purple hairs.
V. lychnitis has powdery angled stems and strongly veined leaves, thickly hairy beneath, green above. The flowering branches are upward-pointing; flowers may be yellow or white with white filament hairs.
V. pulverulentum has an exceptionally dense coating of greyish white meal, which is easily rubbed off. The inflorescence branching is pyramidal, more widespread than in *V. lychnitis*; flowers are bright yellow, filament hairs white.

Spotted Rock-rose *Tuberaria guttata* CISTACEAE
A.4–7. 5–30cm. S. and W. Europe to British Isles (rare).
Early in the morning, this dainty plant lifts its pale yellow, chocolate-spotted flowers to the sun, but very few remain beyond mid-day. Variable in habit, the tallest plants are straggly, the small ones compact. They favour short grassland and sunny sandy places. A basal leaf rosette usually withers by flowering time; stem leaves are small, in opposite pairs; the flat 5-petalled flowers grow in lax, leafless clusters on slender stems.

Corn Marigold *Chrysanthemum segetum* COMPOSITAE
A.6–10. 20–50cm. Most of Europe. Arable weed.
The Corn Marigold is much less common in cornfields today, although its large golden flowers sometimes still transform stubble into a blaze of autumnal glory. Erect stems are branched, with scattered, small, slightly toothed leaves; the larger lower leaves are deeply cut. The composite inflorescences include a central disc of densely packed tubular perfect flowers inside a circlet of bright yellow ray florets.

Navelwort *Umbilicus rupestris* CRASSULACEAE
P.5–8. 10–40cm. S. and W. Europe. Cliffs, roadsides, walls.
Known commonly as Wall Pennywort, this plant has rounded, scalloped leaves, mostly basal. The long stalks are attached to the leaf centres. Rooted in cracks and crevices, the upturned flowering stems hold tall slender inflorescences. Numerous, stalked, greenish cream flowers, subtended by small leafy bracts, droop from leafless upper stems; each flower has 5 sepals around a 5-partite, narrowly tubular corolla.

Asphodel *Asphodelus albus* LILIACEAE
P.4–8. To 1m. S. and C. Europe to N.W. France. Not British.
Asphodels (of mythological Elysian Fields) grow in quantity locally, in rough earthly meadowland, from Mediterranean sea level to 1700m in mountain pastures. This species has numerous large starry flowers in long compact spikes with few or no side branches. The short-stalked flowers have 6 white petals with brown mid-veins and are subtended by brown bracts. The spike is surrounded by basal sharply pointed leaves, about half the plant's full height.

Pale Flax *Linum bienne* LINACEAE
A, B or P.5–8. 20–60cm. S. and W. Europe to British Isles.
This frail-looking plant has a variable life-span; individual flowers are short-lived, but constant replacement ensures a long season. Growing in loose branched clusters, they have 5 pointed sepals and 5 pale lilac-blue petals and green capsules. Leaves are small, linear and sessile on fine flexuous stems. The related *L. usitatissimum*, with larger bluer flowers, has now replaced it in linen production.

Spreading Bellflower *Campanula patula* CAMPANULACEAE
B or P.7–9. 20–60cm. Most Europe. Shady woods, hedgebanks.

Harebell *Campanula rotundifolia* CAMPANULACEAE
P.6–10. 15–40cm. Most of Europe. Locally common.

Flax-leaved Bellflower *Campanula recta* CAMPANULACEAE
P.6–8. 10–35cm. Endemic to Pyrenees; S. and C. France.
Amongst Europe's most spectacularly beautiful wild plants are the numerous species of *Campanula*, some quite distinctive, many very local. They are characterised by showy inflorescences of blue (occasionally white or yellow) flowers, with 5 petals united in a wide funnel or bell-shaped tube. Inside are 5 stamens and a single style, topped by a 3- or 5-lobed stigma, reminiscent of a bell's clapper. The calyx is usually 5-pointed (10-pointed in a few species) and fused with the round green ovary below the corolla. Leaves vary in size and shape between and even within species—a feature to watch in identification.
C. patula has violet-blue flowers, held erect on slender stalks in a branched spreading inflorescence, each bell widely funnel-shaped with outspread, triangular, pointed lobes. Upper leaves small, narrow; lower obovate.
C. rotundifolia has delicate china-blue flowers, familiar from dunes, downs and roadsides to mountain ledges. The name '*rotundifolia*' means round-leaved; look for these at the base of the plants.
C. recta resembles Harebell, but its thick clusters of flowers are dark blue and stem leaves only *c.* 1mm wide. Basal leaves are stalked, toothed, varying in size and shape from fairly long to almost round.

Cornflower *Centaurea cyanus* COMPOSITAE
A.6–8. 20–60cm. All of Europe. Cornfields, waysides. Local.
Once a common cornfield weed, the glorious blue of the Cornflower is now rarely seen in quantity. Branching slender stems and narrow sessile leaves are cottony-grey; involucral bracts below the inflorescence are conspicuously fringed, silvery below, brown above. Each solitary flower head consists of a central disc of small flowers with purplish stamens and white stigmas, encircled by larger brilliant blue florets, tubular with 5 deeply cut spreading lobes.

Sheep's-bit *Jasione montana* CAMPANULACEAE
B.6–9. 5–50cm. Most of Europe. Dry grass, dunes, rocks. Calcifuge.
Although initially so unlike *Campanula*, the rounded, beautiful flower heads of *Jasione* are really tight clusters of tiny mauve-blue bellflowers, with 5 narrow star-spreading petals, a protruding long blue style with 2 blue stigmas and 5 creamy stamens inside. Dying inflorescences are brown. The finely hairy plants are variable in size and branching.

Field Eryngo *Eryngium campestre* UMBELLIFERAE
P.6–9. 30–60cm. Most of Europe, except N. Dry grassy places.
This rigid spiny plant displays its large prickly-lobed basal leaves from spring to autumn on rough dry grassland. The flowering stems are frequently and stiffly branched, with small green terminal flower heads above spreading circles of long, narrow, sharply pointed bracts. The densely packed flowers are sessile, tiny (2–3mm), pale purple to white, interspersed with spiny bracteoles, 2–3 times longer.

Broomrape *Orobanche caryophyllacea* OROBANCHACEAE
A to P.6–7. 15–40cm. Most of Europe, from Denmark S.
This parasite of the roots of Rubiaceae (Bedstraws) is also called Clove-scented Broomrape because of its distinctive perfume. The stiffly erect stem is unbranched, hairy, yellowish purple, with small scales and carries a loose spike of large similarly coloured flowers. Typically, the corolla is tubular and 2-lipped: the upper arched, the lower spreading and 3-lobed; it is hairy with purple stigma lobes.

Common Poppy *Papaver rhoeas* PAPAVERACEAE
A.5–9. To 60cm. Most of Europe. Cornfields, waste ground.
The brilliant scarlet flowers of cornfield poppies emerge from bristly, 2-sepalled buds in summer-long profusion, their large petals frequently with black centres. Numerous dark-anthered stamens surround the pistil, crowned with 8–12 rayed stigmas. Quantities of fine seeds are later dispersed through small holes in the capsule and can remain viable for years, until suitable conditions for growth occur.

Pheasant's-eye *Adonis flammea* RANUNCULACEAE
A.5–7. 10–30cm. C and S. Europe. Not British.

Spring Adonis *Adonis vernalis* RANUNCULACEAE
P.4–5. 10–40cm. Most of Europe, except N. Not British.
The genus *Adonis* has exceptionally finely dissected leaves with narrow lobes, 2–3 times pinnate. Some species have so many leaves that they resemble dense concentrations of small conifers. They are herbaceous, frequently annual, arable weeds with conspicuous red or (more rarely) yellow flowers, solitary on each leafy stem.
A. flammea has delicate fern-like leaves, spreading distinctly and separately from the stem joints, with one large rich scarlet flower well above. Sepals, usually 5, are hairy and not outspread. 8 or so pointed petals, narrow and not overlapping, contrast sharply with the dark centres of stamens, styles and black petal-blotches.
A. vernalis has large golden flowers with overlapping petals; sepals, green in bud, yellowish later, are much shorter. Numerous stems, thickly clothed with bright green leaves, form compact bushy plants, topped by mingled bursting buds, wide-open flowers (the oldest with petals gradually fading to white) and green knobby hard-packed seed heads.

Field Bindweed *Convolvulus arvensis* CONVOLVULACEAE
P.5–10. 20–75cm. All Europe. Cultivated and waste land.
All Bindweeds are beautiful, but some, including this one, are persistent weeds in cultivated land, difficult to eradicate because of deep-growing rhizomes. Long slender stems scramble or climb anti-clockwise around low-growing stronger plants, smothering them with shallow-lobed, arrow-like leaves and charming little pink and white funnel-flowers, sometimes with maroon-blotched centres.

Wild Strawberry *Fragaria vesca* ROSACEAE
P.5–7. 5–30cm. All Europe. Hedgerows, grassy banks.
The Wild Strawberry produces long runners with new plants rooting at the nodes. 3-lobed leaves are silky hairy beneath; white flowers arise separately from the plant's centre. Flowers and fruits often appear together, the fruit at first green, then red, with small hard seeds lightly embedded on the soft surface.

Everlasting-pea *Lathyrus latifolius* LEGUMINOSAE
P.6–8. 1–2m. S. Europe. Naturalised elsewhere. Hedges, banks.
The resemblance between this plant and the cultivated Sweet-pea is strongly marked as it pulls up its rich carmine-pink 'butterfly' flowers over hedgerow shrubs by means of slender tendrils. These grow from between the paired, broadly elliptic leaves, which vary from 4–15cm long. The leaf stalks and main stems are smooth and broadly winged; flowers are borne in loose clusters.

Large Purple Stork's-bill *Erodium manescavi* GERANIACEAE
P.6–8. 20–40cm. C., W. Pyrenees. Grassy places. Not British.
Leaves and flower stalks arise separately and directly from the root stock to produce handsome bushy plants. All green parts are hairy. The large pinnate leaves have deeply indented leaflets and the clustered flowers radiate from a circle of bracts on stalks of varying lengths. 5 narrow, sharply pointed sepals alternate with 5 rounded, vividly purple petals, attractively patterned with darker veins and pale central patches. Long narrow seed pods provide the 'stork's bills'.

Hare's-foot Clover *Trifolium arvense* LEGUMINOSAE
A.5–10. To 40cm. All of Europe. Sandy fields, dunes.
The most noticeable and attractive feature of this small clover is the soft furry seed head, from which many national names are derived including the English one. The tiny pale pink flowers are almost enclosed within much longer hairy calyx teeth, which later elongate around each small hard seed, producing the typical rounded-oblong 'hare's foot'. The mat-forming plants are completely hairy with narrow-lobed trifoliate leaves.

Dandelion *Taraxacum officinale* COMPOSITAE
P.3–12. 10–30cm. All of Europe. Roadsides, fields, lawns.
Although the golden-flowered dandelion is a garden pest, how gaily it brightens many a roadside and the perfect symmetry of its parachute seed heads or 'clocks', so readily blown away, is fascinating. The tap root is difficult to eradicate and, if merely broken, produces new plants. Backward-pointing leaf lobes are variable in shape; all florets are rayed and perfect in structure.

Sneezewort *Achillea ptarmica* COMPOSITAE
P.6–9. 20–60cm. Most of Europe. Damp meadows, streamsides.
The daisy-like flowers of Sneezewort grow in loose, almost flat-topped clusters at the head of erect leafy stems, branched only near the top. The sessile leaves are linear, with evenly toothed margins, up to 8cm long. Each inflorescence, up to 2cm across, consists of an inner pad of greenish white disc florets, encircled by broad white ray florets; both types produce fertile seeds. A sneezing powder is made from the crushed dried leaves.

Colt's-foot *Tussilago farfara* COMPOSITAE
P.2–7. 10–25cm. All of Europe. Waste ground to 2600m.
Colt's-Foot is one of the most widespread of European plants, favouring damp sticky ground—often clayey and recently disturbed—from eroded sea cliffs through rubbish tips and roadside rubble to glacial moraines where, at a height of 2600m, the bright yellow flowers contrast delight-fully with the purple Alpine Soldanellas. In early spring, the composite inflorescences appear, before the large heart-shaped shallow-lobed leaves. These heads of massed florets are solitary and terminal on short, brownish, scaly stalks, which lengthen and droop after flowering, becoming erect again when the silky-plumed seeds develop above the then reflexed involucral bracts. The leaves, usually green above, but felted with hairs below, are the source of a valuable medicinal relief for chest complaints, hence the name '*Tussilago*' from the Latin '*tussis*', meaning a cough.

Cowslip *Primula veris* PRIMULACEAE
P.4–5. 10–25cm. Most of Europe. Grassland, chiefly calcareous.
Golden Cowslip flowers, widely scattered over cliffs, downs, pastures and ancient earthworks, are most welcome heralds of summer. Several large crinkled leaves, with blades abruptly narrowed at the base, encircle a few longer flowering stems which carry terminal umbels of pendant scented flowers. Each pale green calyx tube surrounds a yellow tubular corolla of 5 slightly spreading notched petals with darker yellow inner centres.

Large Snapdragon *Antirrhinum latifolium* SCROPHULARIACEAE
P.4–11. 20–100cm. C. Italy to N.E. Spain. Endemic. Not British.
This beautiful plant adorns rocky cliffs and stony roadsides, although infrequently. Several erect leafy stems end in racemes of large, erect creamy yellow flowers with broadly tubular bilabiate corollas. The paler upper lip is pink-veined within; the lower bright yellow outside and cream inside, with yellow lines and fine white hairs. Stems, leaves and sepals are softly hairy; the broad oval leaves are characteristic.

Large Yellow Ox-eye *Telekia speciosa* COMPOSITAE
P.6–8. To 2m. C. and E. Europe. Not British.
This is similar to the more widespread Elecampane, *Inula helenium*. Both are erect, robust and somewhat hairy, with numerous very large leaves, the lower stalked, the upper sessile. The centre of the sunflower-like inflorescence is packed with perfect disc florets, surrounded by numerous, long, narrow, orange-yellow ray florets. The involucre is cup-shaped with rows of leafy bracts.

Oxford Ragwort *Senecio squalidus* COMPOSITAE
A, B or P.4–11. To 30cm. S. Italy, Sicily. Naturalised elsewhere.
This remarkable plant has loosely clustered yellow inflorescences with black-tipped bracts and numerous, irregularly lobed toothed leaves. It ranges from the volcanic ash of Mount Etna and Vesuvius to urban wasteland further north. Originally imported into botanic gardens in the 18th century, it has become established in towns, and is especially colourful along rail routes and on bombed sites.

Silverweed *Potentilla anserina* ROSACEAE
P.5–7. To 20cm. Most of Europe; not Mediterranean. Verges, waste ground, dunes.
Silverweed has a thick covering of silky silvery hairs beneath the pinnately lobed serrated leaves. The large, golden, 5-petalled, rose-like flowers are held singly and erect above them. Large leaf lobes alternate with very small ones, all usually green above. Long reddish runners (to 80cm) creep above ground, producing new plants—roots, leaves and flowering stems—at frequent intervals.

Creeping-Jenny *Lysimachia nummularia* PRIMULACEAE
P.5–8. To 60cm. All Europe. Damp meadows, hedgebanks; local.
The long trailing stems of this plant spread over the ground, rooting at the nodes and producing dense mats of shining bright green leaves, whose rounded shape give it the alternative name of Moneywort. The leaves grow in pairs, as do the vivid yellow flowers, which have 5 pointed sepals alternating with 5 spreading petals, united below and with glandular dots. Opposite the petals are 5 stamens, encircling a single style and stigma.

Lesser Celandine *Ranunculus ficaria* RANUNCULACEAE
P.2–5. 5–25cm. All of Europe. Meadows, hedgebanks, woods.
This bright messenger of spring spreads masses of glossy golden flowers over moist ground for several weeks. From the root stock arise flowering stems and many long-stalked leaves, heart-shaped, dark green and smooth. The solitary terminal flowers have only 3 sepals and 7–12 petals, shining yellow above, greenish below. Wide open in sunshine, they close at dusk and become whitish with age.

Common Iris *Iris germanica* IRIDACEAE
P.3–5. 40–90cm. Most of Europe, except N. Not British.
The origin of *Iris germanica* is doubtful. A hybrid, cultivated over the centuries for perfume and beauty, it is now widely naturalised in stony grassy places. The leaves are typically sword-like and the few large showy flowers, borne on an erect glabrous stem, have erect, broad, velvety, blue-purple 'standards' (3) and drooping 'falls' (3) with yellow 'beards' at the throat.

Bittersweet *Solanum dulcamara* SOLANACEAE
P.6–9. To 6m. All Europe. Hedges, woods, waste ground.
The long trailing stems of this plant, also called Woody Nightshade, scramble over other vegetation. The stalked leaves generally have 1 large and 2 small lobes; the loosely clustered flowers have 5 vivid purple petals, spreading or reflexed around 5 protruding golden anthers. It is not the true Deadly Nightshade, but its bright red berries can cause severe illness and should never be eaten.

Red Campion *Silene dioica* CARYOPHYLLACEAE
B or P.5–7. 30–60cm. Most of Europe. Hedgerows, woods, locally abundant.
Red Campion is erect, hairy, with broad leaves in opposite pairs and deep pink flowers on short side branches. The 5-pointed calyx and corolla are both tubular, the latter with 5 large, spreading, deeply notched petals; at their base are tiny scales forming a central frill, surrounding either 5 styles and stigmas or 10 stamens as the flowers are unisexual.

Russian Comfrey *Symphytum × uplandicum* BORAGINACEAE
P.5–8. To 2m. N.W. Europe. Naturalised. Roadsides.
Comfreys are roughly hairy plants with arching inflorescences of numerous pendant bell-like flowers. This is a hybrid between *S. asperum* and the widespread Common Comfrey, *S. officinale*. Russian Comfrey is distinguished by its leaves, which are neither cordate nor strongly winged, its intensely blue flowers and its usually drier habitat. The flowers of *S. officinale*, common near water, are cream and purple.

Blue Bugle *Ajuga genevensis* LABIATAE
P.5–7. To 30cm. C. and S.E. Europe. Extinct in British Isles.
Crowded, erect flowering stems, growing from an underground creeping rhizome, clothe the ground with massed whorled spikes of vivid dark blue. Square-stalked stems and oval leaves are hairy; short-stalked stem leaves grow in opposite pairs; basal leaves are larger and long-stalked, but wither by flowering time. The flowers, in the axils of short bluish bracts, have a very small upper lip and a larger 3-lobed lower one.

Venus's-looking-glass *Legousia speculum-veneris* CAMPANULACEAE
A.6–7. To 30cm. Much of Europe, except N. Not British.
These unmistakable vividly purple flowers bloom along the margins of arable fields. 1–2cm across, they cluster loosely on short side branches arising from the axils of sessile simple leaves. 5 broad petals spread flat from a very short tube, alternating with 5 narrow sepals; the centres are white with green blotches; flowers are occasionally white.

Germander Speedwell *Veronica chamaedrys* SCROPHULARIACEAE
P.5–7. To 30cm. All Europe. Hedgerows, grassy places.
This is one of the most attractive of a large varied genus, characterised by 4-petalled (3 large, 1 small) flowers possessing only 2 stamens. Its erect stems have 2 distinctly separate rows of white hairs and crenate, slightly cordate, leaves in opposite pairs. The beautiful bright blue flowers grow in lax racemes from the upper leaf axils, white-centred and dark-veined inside, paler blue outside.

Teasel *Dipsacus fullonum* DIPSACACEAE
B.7–9. 60–180cm. Most Europe; not mts and far N. Waste land.
Teasel's persistent bristly spikes are fascinatingly peculiar, especially when ringed by purple florets, tightly packed between small bracts, the whole encircled by long narrow ones, all very spiny. The stiff branching stems and the lower surface of leaf mid-ribs are spiny; stem leaves are sessile, in pairs; radical leaves wither by flowering time. It is related to the similar cultivated *D. sativus* whose *hooked* inflorescence spines were used for 'teasing' the surface of woollen cloth.

Greater Burdock *Arctium lappa* COMPOSITAE
B.6–9. 90–130cm. All Europe. Waysides, waste places.
Best known at seeding time, Burdock has a stout furrowed reddish stem, exceptionally large, long-stalked basal leaves, cottony beneath like the stem leaves, and branching clusters of rounded spiky inflorescences. The tubular purple florets show paler protruding styles and stigmas when mature. They are surrounded by overlapping greenish bracts with incurving hooked tips, which later become brown and stiff and readily cling to the coats of animals and clothing for dispersal.

Jersey Thrift *Armeria alliacea* PLUMBAGINACEAE
P.5–9. 15–40cm. C. and S. Europe, Jersey.
Like the related *A. maritima* (p. 28), this lovely pink-buttoned plant forms carpets of tufted growth, but inland, sometimes locally abundant. Usually much taller than *A. maritima*, with comparatively broad, flat, pointed leaves, to 12cm long, each with 3–7 veins (*A. maritima* usually has 1). Both produce several flowering stems topped by a solitary, rounded, dense inflorescence of many small tubular flowers.

Alpine Bistort *Polygonum viviparum* POLYGONACEAE
P.6–8. 6–30cm. Arctic and N. Europe; also mountains.

Common Bistort *Polygonum bistorta* POLYGONACEAE
P.6–9. 25–50cm. Much of Europe, except N. Widespread.
These 2 species of *Polygonum* have several characters in common: their stems are erect, slender, glabrous, with a few sessile leaves, smaller than the stalked basal ones; flowers, usually pink with protruding stamens and styles, grow in terminal crowded spikes.
P. viviparum has characteristic red bulbils, which replace the flowers of the lower half of the spike. These fall to the ground and reproduce vegetatively. The anthers are purple; all leaves are narrow, glaucous beneath, with inrolled margins.
P. bistorta often produces dense pink sheets of colour in moist meadows and along roadsides. Taller than its relative, with longer, wider flower spikes, it has pale anthers and no bulbils. Radical leaves are broad, especially near the base, with strongly marked mid-ribs.

Hedgerow Crane's bill *Geranium pyrenaicum* GERANIACEAE
P.6–8. 25–75cm. Most of Europe. Meadows, waste ground.

Herb-Robert *Geranium robertianum* GERANIACEAE
A or B.5–8. To 70cm. All Europe. Shady places, hedgerows.
Many Geraniums are very attractive, crowded with palmately divided or lobed leaves and richly coloured flowers of pink, purple or blue. Their characteristic long seed capsules—the 'crane's-bills'—are formed from the elongated persistent styles; when the seeds are ripe, the style splits vertically into 5 narrow lengths which curl upwards from the base, ejecting the seeds as they do so.
G. pyrenaicum grows from sea level to 1900m. The plants are slightly hairy; leaves, from 5–8cm broad, are rounded in outline, with 5 deep, shallowly tri-partite lobes. The 5-petalled flowers are mauve-purple, also deeply lobed. Introduced in northern Europe.
G. robertianum has beautiful fern-like leaves to add to the attraction of its small deep pink flowers. The softly hairy plants are often red-tinged.

Thorn-apple *Datura stramonium* SOLANACEAE
A.7–10. To 1m. All Europe; introduced in N. Waste and
cultivated ground.
This plant, fortunately found only occasionally, is narcotic and poisonous. The seeds can remain dormant for many years, but when land is
disturbed, can quickly produce tall, leafy, strong-smelling plants, with
big white funnel-shaped flowers. Large, green, spiny capsules, about 5cm
long, contain several very poisonous hard black seeds. Guard against
children mistaking these for horse chestnuts.

Round-leaved Restharrow *Ononis rotundifolia* LEGUMINOSAE
P.5–8. 30–50cm. S.W. Europe. Rocky places. Not British.
These compact attractive shrubs flower profusely on stony ground and
rocks by hilly roadsides. The leaves, trifoliate, toothed and with definitely
rounded leaflets, distinguish it from *O. fruticosa*, which has long, fairly
narrow leaflets. Both display masses of beautiful pink 'butterfly' flowers,
from 1–3 in stalked clusters; both are much-branched, glandular-hairy,
but not spiny, as are some Restharrows.

Tassel Hyacinth *Muscari comosum* LILIACEAE
P.4–7. 20–60cm. Mediterranean and C. Europe.

Grape Hyacinth *Muscari atlanticum* LILIACEAE
P.3–5. To 20cm. Most of Europe except N. Grassy places.
These two bulbous plants possess 2 types of flowers, the upper sterile and
the lower fertile, forming a terminal raceme on erect stems, which are
glossy like the linear leaves. Individual flowers are urn-shaped, with short
reflexed lobes at the narrow corolla-opening.
M. comosum is unmistakable with its delightful topknot of rich blue sterile
flowers, an attraction for insects. Below, the fertile flowers grow loosely,
mostly on horizontal stalks, all brownish with paler corolla lobes; the
whole inflorescence may be 20cm long.
M. atlanticum belongs to a distinctive group, but with confused specific
naming. The sterile flowers form a small tight bunch above the very
bright blue fertile ones with white reflexed corolla lobes. They are
frequently cultivated; the glossy linear leaves are at first quite neat but
become straggling as the flowers open in spring time.

Cupidone *Catananche caerulea* COMPOSITAE
P.6–8. 20–90cm. S.W. Europe. Dry grassy places. Not British.
This plant is reminiscent of Chicory, but its leaves are much fewer, very
narrow with a few pointed lobes. Flowers are purple-blue with very dark
centres; only ray florets are present, their straps ending in 5 sharp points.
Stigmas and styles are contrastingly yellow and anther tubes purple. The
distinctive involucral bracts are papery, almost transparent, and sharply
pointed with brown mid-veins.

Lesser Periwinkle *Vinca minor* APOCYNACEAE
P.3–5. 30–60cm. Most of Europe, except N. Hedgebanks,
woodland edges.
From lowlands to about 1320m, the trailing stems of Lesser Periwinkle
occur locally in moist shady places, rooting at intervals and producing
large mats of glossy evergreen leaves with stalked, solitary, misty blue
flowers in the axils. From furled buds, 5 large asymmetric petal lobes
open flat above a short tube. Smaller flowers, more procumbent habit and
hairless calyces distinguish it from the larger *V. major*.

Blue Lettuce *Lactuca perennis* COMPOSITAE
P.5–8. 20–70cm. C. Europe. Rocky, grassy places. Not British.
Similar in habit to Chicory and Cupidone, Blue Lettuce is tall with
outspread branches and blue flowers, but smooth and glaucous with grey-
green stems and leaves. The leaves are deeply pinnately lobed, the lower
stalked, the upper clasping the stem. Inflorescences contain ray florets
only. A milky juice exudes from the cut stems as a distinguishing point.

Common Toadflax *Linaria vulgaris* SCROPHULARIACEAE
P.6–10. 30–80cm. All Europe. Grassy roadsides, waste ground.
Autumn roadsides are cheered by the gay flowers of Toadflax, perhaps so named because of its horizontally wide corolla mouth and its flax-like leaves. Related to *Cymbalaria*, with the same flower structure, it is otherwise very different. Numerous narrow leaves clothe the tall erect stems and the flowers are massed together in long terminal racemes. The corolla's upper lip is pale yellow and the broad lower one has a large throat boss, deep orange-yellow, like the long downward-pointing spur.

Golden-drop *Onosma fastigiata* BORAGINACEAE
B.6–7. 10–30cm. C. and W. France; N.W. Italy. Not British.
Onosmas resemble small plants of the more widespread Comfrey (*Symphytum* spp.) in their often bushy leafy appearance and the possession of a dense covering of white hairs. Several branched flowering stems, with numerous greyish leaves, terminate in curving inflorescences of drooping, pale yellow, tubular flowers, with 5 regular short lobes at the mouth. Although generally similar, this genus exhibits such a wide range of variation, especially in the structure of the hairs, that identification is confusing.

Ivy-leaved Toadflax *Cymbalaria muralis* SCROPHULARIACEAE
P.5–9. 10–80cm. Most of Europe; introduced C. and N.
This charming plant festoons itself in tangled but tidy masses over walls (occasionally rocks), rooting in crevices. Long trailing stems carry numerous ivy-like leaves with spurred bilabiate purple flowers growing singly in the axils. The upper lip is erect, notched and dark-veined, the lower 3-lobed with a yellow and white centre. After flowering, the flexible stalks curve towards the wall to deposit the seeds in cracks, ready for germination.

Purple Viper's-grass *Scorzonera purpurea* COMPOSITAE
P.5–6. 15–45cm. C. and S.E. Europe. Not British.
Like the related Goat's-beards (*Tragopogon* spp.), the flowers of this plant open fully only in sunshine; it grows in fields and grassy places to 2300m. It differs in having several rows of involucral bracts, overlapping and shorter than the florets, instead of a single row of long ones. Leaves are narrow, entire, with sheaths persistent around the bases of the smooth sparsely branched stems. Solitary inflorescences have perfect mauve ray florets of varying lengths.

Dog Rose *Rosa canina* ROSACEAE
P.5–7. 1–3m. All Europe. Hedgerows, thickets, woods.
One of the many wild rose species, this plant is typical of their general structure; a hedgerow scrambler with sharp hooked stem prickles. Pinnately divided leaves have 4 or 6 paired leaflets and a terminal one, all serrate. The large delicate pink or white flowers, usually perfumed, are amongst the best known of all wild blossoms, enriching roadsides throughout the summer. Then follow the equally attractive seed heads—scarlet hips—an excellent source of vitamin C.

Hawthorn *Crataegus monogyna* ROSACEAE
P.5–6. To 5m. All Europe. Thickets, hedges, woods.
The first spring green of bursting Hawthorn buds, soon followed by a thick cloak of white blossom is a delightful picture. Known also as Quickthorn, because of its rapid growth and numerous sharp spines, Hawthorn has been frequently planted to produce almost impenetrable field boundaries. The leaves are numerous, in short-stalked clusters, lobed and serrate, almost glabrous. The nearly flat-topped inflorescences are strongly sweet-scented and include about 16 flowers, with 5 petals, and several stamens with pink anthers surrounding a single style. The decorative crimson haws which follow provide good food for wintering birds.

Foxglove *Digitalis purpurea* SCROPHULARIACEAE
B.6–8. 50–150cm. N., C. and S.W. Europe. Widespread.

Small Yellow Foxglove *Digitalis lutea* SCROPHULARIACEAE
P.6–8. 45–60cm. W. and C. Europe. Endemic. Not British.
The handsome spikes of Foxgloves grow from rosettes of large, stalked simple leaves. The upper stem leaves are smaller and subtend the flattened tubular flowers. These open from the lowest upwards; all stages from buds to capsules occur on a unilateral inflorescence. Each flower has 4 stamens and 1 style with a 2-lobed stigma; the style lengthens later, remaining on the rounded green seed capsule.
D. purpurea is locally abundant in woods and hedgerows on lime-free soil. Flowers are large, purplish red, occasionally white, spotted inside. Though poisonous, it yields the valuable heart drug, digitalin.
D. lutea has finely serrate shining leaves and small, pale yellow, unspotted flowers. Local in calcareous woods and roadside banks to sub-alpine regions. Poisonous.

Lily-of-the-valley *Convallaria majalis* LILIACEAE
P.5–6. 8–20cm. Most of Europe. Woods, scrub to about 1550m.
Well known, frequently cultivated, and great favourites, these charming flowers scent woodland and shady scrub with an exquisite perfume. About 10, white, 6-lobed flower bells form a pendant unilateral raceme on a slender curving stem, all overshadowed by 2 large shining radical leaves. Evidence of berries we rarely see, probably due to the flowers being gathered; fortunately the possession of spreading rhizomes helps the plants to survive. Protected in Switzerland.

White Helleborine *Cephalanthera damasonium* ORCHIDACEAE
P. 5–7. 15–50cm. Much of Europe, especially C. and S.
Woods, calcareous.
Growing amongst the undergrowth and shade of beech woods, the creamy flowering spikes of this orchid produce a somewhat ghostly effect. The few flowers are erect in the axils of long leafy bracts and rarely open widely enough to display the yellow markings on the small heart-shaped lip. Leaves are broad and spirally arranged around the stem, differing from the related *C. longifolia* which has 2 rows of stiff narrow leaves.

Yellow Pimpernel *Lysimachia nemorum* PRIMULACEAE
P.5–8. To 40cm long. W. and C. Europe. Damp shady places.
Moist woodlands are the home of this attractive plant, which provides a carpet of fresh green leaves and bright yellow starry flowers through most of the summer. From the procumbent main stem grow several short erect shoots, all with numerous pairs of broadly oval leaves; the upper ones subtend the long-stalked flowers. These possess 5 small sepals alternating with 5 broad petals, with a stamen opposite each one.

Yellow Star-of-Bethlehem *Gagea lutea* LILIACEAE
P.4–6. 8–25cm. Most of Europe. Damp woods and pastures.
These rather inconspicuous Bethlehem Stars hide in moist shady places. Only 1 leaf is produced, directly from the bulb, hairless, ribbed, much longer than the single flowering stem, often strongly curved. Though yellow within, the few 6-petalled flowers are dulled by green lines outside and grow in 1 or 2 loose clusters, subtended by 2 bracts; one small and one overtopping the delicate flower stalks.

Green Hellebore *Helleborus viridis* RANUNCULACEAE
P.3–5. 20–40cm. Endemic. W. and C. Europe. Woods, thickets. Local.
This fascinating relative of the Christmas-rose is distinguished by its intensely green flowers in slightly drooping, loose clusters. In each flower, 5 large green petal-like sepals encircle about 10 very small flattened tubular nectaries which are modified petals. Numerous creamy stamens surround 3 or 4 pistils. The large green seed pods persist for some time. Most leaves are basal, stalked, large and palmately divided.

Holly *Ilex aquifolium* AQUIFOLIACEAE
P.5–6. To 15m. Most of Europe. Woods, thickets, hedges.
Holly is a firm favourite; its brilliant scarlet berries and shining, evergreen, spiny leaves decorate many a Christmas gathering and any berries left provide winter food for birds. The flowers are small, white and inconspicuous, in clusters almost hidden by the dense foliage. It is frequently, but not always, unisexual. Protected in Switzerland.

Butcher's-broom *Ruscus aculeatus* LILIACEAE
P.1–4. 30–100cm. Most of Europe, except E. Dry woods.
Easily overlooked because of its dull dark green appearance, this peculiar un-lily-like shrub has numerous stiff striate branches, once used as brooms, covered with thick leaf-like growths tipped with pale spines. They are not true leaves, but modified branchlets, with tiny, greenish, purple-dotted flowers on the upper surface. Male and female flowers are separate; the latter produce large bright red berries (10–15mm).

Ivy *Hedera helix* ARALIACEAE
P.Fl. 9–11. Frt 1–4. To 30m. Most of Europe; rare E. Woods.
Ivy frequently carpets woodlands with procumbent stems and shining lobed leaves or climbs trees by means of small adhesive aerial rootlets on its woody stems; it also thrives on town walls and buildings. Small green flowers provide insects with the last nectar of the year and the ripe black berries give birds their first food of the year.

Wedge-leaved Saxifrage *Saxifraga cuneifolia* SAXIFRAGACEAE
P.6–8. 10–30cm. Pyrenees to Carpathians. Sub-alpine woods. Not British.
Characteristic of mossy bouldery shade, this dainty plant is sometimes locally abundant. 8–12, wedge-shaped, slightly dentate leaves grow in basal rosettes, green and smooth above, purplish below; they later become brown and persistent, so that up to 5 rosettes may be found, one above the other, on one plant. The small delicate flowers are numerous on thin branching stems, each with 5 narrow white petals splashed with yellow at the centre.

Angular Solomon's-seal *Polygonatum odoratum* LILIACEAE
P.5–6. 20–35cm. Most of Europe. Local. Woods, shady places.
This and *P. multiflorum* are similar; both have long arching stems above which numerous large oval-pointed leaves, sessile and slightly glaucous, are borne almost erect. Greenish cream tubular flowers hang below the stem. This plant is distinguished by having only 1 or 2 scented straight-sided flowers on each separate slender stalk. They are followed by bluish black berries. The twisted angled stems smell of freshly picked peas when broken.

Wood-sorrel *Oxalis acetosella* OXALIDACEAE
P.4–5. 5–15cm. Most of Europe. Woods, shady areas; to 2100m.
Leaves and flowers of Wood-sorrel grow from a creeping rhizome, singly and separately, on stalks of almost equal length. Fresh green, 3-lobed leaves carpet deciduous woodlands; at sundown the lobes fold together, inwards and downwards. The delicate cup-shaped flowers have 5 petals, white, finely streaked with purple, occasionally pink, yellow-centred. Small green sepals, styles and stigmas each number 5, stamens 10.

Spurge-laurel *Daphne laureola* THYMELAEACEAE
P.2–4. 40–100cm. Mainly S., W. and C. Europe. Local.
An inconspicuous, evergreen, flowering shrub of usually calcareous woodlands, with sparsely branched stems carrying rather crowded, dark green, glossy, leathery leaves, simple, ovate and about 5–12cm long. In the upper axils grow short-stalked, few-flowered clusters of small tubular green flowers, which are 4-partite with no separate sepals and petals. They secrete nectar and, after insect pollination, produce oval black berries, bitter and poisonous like the bark.

Common Twayblade *Listera ovata* ORCHIDACEAE
P.5–7. 30–45cm. Most of Europe. Woods, hedgerows, grassland.
Recorded as Europe's commonest wild Orchid, Twayblade is widespread
in many habitats, often abundant in moist woodlands. Though inconspicuous, it is the largest 2-leaved green orchid; leaves, 5–20cm long,
oval, strongly veined are opposite on the lower stem. A long loose raceme
bears many small flowers, green, sometimes red-tinged; 5 tiny upper
petals form a hood; the long hanging lip is deeply 2-lobed.

Spiked Rampion *Phyteuma spicatum* CAMPANULACEAE
P.5–7. 30–70cm. Widespread much of Europe.
The long, tight, unbranched spikes of this pale yellow Rampion unfold
from the base. Each flower, at first a curved cylindrical tube, splits
centrally into 5 strips, united at the top and base. Finally, the tips separate
into narrow spreading petals; which, with the protruding styles and
stigmas give the spikes their shaggy appearance. Leaves are long-
triangular, crenate: the upper ones sessile, the lower long-stalked.

Oxlip *Primula elatior* PRIMULACEAE
P.3–6. 10–25cm. Most of Europe. Lowlands to 2500m.
The splendid beauty of the Oxlip is displayed prolifically, but locally
in lowland woods and hedgerows and on snow-patterned mountain
slopes, wherever moist ground prevails. Leaves are all radical, crinkled,
downy and finely toothed, with blades narrowing suddenly into rather
short stalks. The few flowering stems are leafless, lightly hairy, with
somewhat 1-sided terminal clusters of drooping pale yellow primrose-like
flowers with darker centres, about 2cm across.

Cow-wheat *Melampyrum nemorosum* SCROPHULARIACEAE
A.6–8. 20–40cm. Much of Europe. Mountains. Not British.
A brilliant display is given by this unusual plant, whose erect branched
stems terminate in a glorious mixture of purple and gold. Tubular
orange-yellow flowers grow in pairs in the axils of leafy bracts which are
toothed at the base and graduate from dark green below to royal purple
above. A semi-parasite, the plant becomes locally dominant at the
expense of other vegetation, providing dense masses of colour.

Wild Daffodil *Narcissus pseudonarcissus* AMARYLLIDACEAE
P.3–5. 20–35cm. W. Europe. Endemic. Sometimes naturalised.
Sometimes abundant on damp ground in deciduous woodlands and on
steep grassy mountain slopes, the gay flowers of Daffodils light the way
from winter into spring. The large solitary flowers, on glabrous, flattened
stalks, emerge from thin papery sheaths. 6 spreading outer petals are paler
than and about as long as the inner golden corona with its irregular frilly
rim; inside are 6 stamens and a single style and stigma.

Primrose *Primula vulgaris* PRIMULACEAE
P.12–5. 5–12cm. W., C. and S.W. Europe. Moist shady places.
Another springtime favourite, these large pale yellow flowers provide the
classic example of the heterostylous forms of many Primulas: 'pin-eyed'
with pistil visible at the throat and 5 stamens below, and 'thrum-eyed'
with positions reversed. The large crinkled leaf blades narrow gradually
downwards, making a delightful spreading background for the central
nosegay of slender-stalked flowers (3cm across), both arising together
from ground level.

Lady's-slipper *Cypripedium calceolus* ORCHIDACEAE
P.5–7. 15–50cm. Local, rare, decreasing; to 2000m.
Europe's largest and most magnificent Orchid is found occasionally in
calcareous woodland and on steep sub-alpine slopes. A single erect stem
carries 3–4, broad, furrowed leaves and 1–2 large, strikingly beautiful
flowers. 4 maroon petals, pointed, flexible and sometimes twisted,
surround and protect the lip, or shining yellow 'slipper', and the column,
or reproductive organs, above its opening. Legally protected.

No English name *Aruncus dioicus* ROSACEAE
P.5–8. To 2m. Woods in mountains to 1700m. Not British.
This attractive shrub has feathery masses of creamy white flowers and very large fern-like leaves. These are 2 or 3 times pinnately divided into several leaflets, oval, acute, sharply serrate and with prominent veins; lobes to 17cm long. The foamy appearance of the long much-branched inflorescences is due to the large numbers of tiny, 5-petalled, rose-like flowers, each with numerous projecting stamens.

Baneberry *Actaea spicata* RANUNCULACEAE
P.5–7. 30–60cm. Much of Europe. Calcareous woods, to 1900m.
Baneberry has large decorative ferny leaves, subdivided into numerous, lobed, toothed leaflets. Flowering racemes arise from the upper axils on long stalks; small white flowers usually have 4 short-lived sepals and petals and several prominent white stamens. Oval green ovaries, 1 per flower, develop into shining black berries in conspicuous attractive clusters. Like the whole plant they are very poisonous!

Toothwort *Lathraea squamaria* OROBANCHACEAE
P.3–5. 8–30cm. Most of Europe. Parasitic on woodland trees.
Small clusters of strange whitish plants grow around the bases of trees such as Hazel, Beech and Elm. These are the parasitic plants of Toothwort, which obtain their sustenance from these tree roots and therefore possess no chlorophyll. Sturdy and squat, their dense unilateral racemes of drooping, lightly purple-tinged, tubular flowers are normal, with calyx, bilabiate corolla, 4 stamens and a long style with protruding stigma.

Bird's-nest Orchid *Neottia nidus-avis* ORCHIDACEAE
P.6–7. 20–50cm. Most of Europe; rare extreme N. Humus-rich woods.
Like Toothwort, this yellow-brown orchid lacks chlorophyll but it differs by absorbing nutriment from decayed plant and animal material, i.e. it is a saprophyte. The erect stems have pale brown terminal racemes of typical orchid flowers, with fused stamens and pistil and a long pendant deeply 2-lobed lip. These characters distinguish *Neottia* from the superficially similar parasitic Broomrapes. Dead flowering stems frequently persist to the following year.

Ramsons *Allium ursinum* LILIACEAE
P.4–6. 10–45cm. Most of Europe; rarer in N.E. Damp woods.
The attraction of these white starry flowers is offset by the strong odour of onions wafting from the large bright green leaves. They often dominate extensive areas of deciduous woodland to the almost complete exclusion of other plants. From each bulb, a single erect, glossy triangular stem terminates in a cluster of stalked 6-petalled flowers, spreading above the split papery sheath which protected them in bud.

Wood Anemone *Anemone nemorosa* RANUNCULACEAE
P.3–5. 6–30cm. Most of Europe. Abundant in deciduous woods.
The slender flowering stems of Wood Anemones or Windflowers are encircled midway by 3, finely cut, 3-lobed leaves, resembling the larger radical leaves which follow the flowers. Terminal and solitary, the flowers have no green sepals, but 5–9 spreading petals, pink outside, white within; numerous golden stamens surround a central group of pistils, which develop into a knob of hard green seeds.

Snowdrop *Galanthus nivalis* AMARYLLIDACEAE
P.1–3. 10–25cm. Most Europe, not N. Often naturalised.
Snowdrops are the first flowers of the year to appear in abundance, their pure whiteness contrasting with the slim blue-green stalks and leaves. The flowers droop singly from thin arched stalks, protected at first by a papery sheath. After opening, 3 outer petals spread around an inner circlet of 3 shorter ones, striped boldly green inside and showing green crescents below the tips outside.

Early-purple Orchid *Orchis mascula* ORCHIDACEAE
P.4–7. 15–30cm. Much of Europe. Widespread, common.
A variable species, the leaves may be clear green or, more often, distinctly marked with dark spots; flowers shade from white through pink to typical rich deep purple. Identification is helped by their early flowering and preference for calcareous woods and pastures. The flower lip has 3 spreading lobes and a white spotted centre; 3 petals form a hood and the remaining 2 are characteristically almost erect.

Bastard Balm *Melittis melisophyllum* LABIATAE
P.5–7. To 50cm. Much of Europe, except N. Woods, hedges.
This attractive plant of semi-shade is square-stemmed and lightly hairy, with several pairs of egg-shaped, dark green, crenate leaves, in the upper axils of which grow 1-sided clusters of 2–6 large flowers. Shading from white to deep pink, these are tubular and bilabiate; the lower 3-lobed lip is larger than the upper rounded one; 4 stamens and the style project slightly beyond the corolla's throat.

White Wood Crane's-bill *Geranium sylvaticum* ssp. *rivulare* GERANIACEAE
P.6–8. 30–50cm. W. Alps. Endemic, local; to 2400m. Not British.
This pale-flowered Crane's-bill decorates shady mountain streamsides, rocks and light woodland in scattered colonies. The stems are erect, slightly hairy and leafy; both these and larger radical leaves are palmately lobed almost to the base and deeply irregularly dentate. Delicate flowers grow in pairs on long thin stalks in the upper leaf axils; the 5 fragile petals are white with purple lines; 10 purple anthers surround the single pistil.

Wood Vetch *Vicia sylvatica* LEGUMINOSAE
P.6–8. 1–2m. Most of Europe. Chiefly mountain woods.
This dainty Vetch straggles up and over shrubby vegetation by using fine but strong, sensitive, branched tendrils. These replace the terminal leaflets on the numerous pinnate leaves, which each have about 16 sessile lateral leaflets. Typical leguminous flowers hang in long 1-sided clusters; soft purple to white shades mingle on the erect, dark-veined standard and wings, and the white purple-tipped keel.

Knotted Crane's-bill *Geranium nodosum* GERANIACEAE
P.5–9. 20–50cm. Mountains, S. Europe. Endemic to 1600m. Not British.
Local and rare, this lovely species is distinguished by its leaves, unusually solid for a *Geranium*. The typical palmate division occurs about quarter-way from the base; though irregularly crenate-dentate, they are not further lobed. Flower petals are deep pinkish lilac with violet veins, broad and notched. Seed capsules of both this and *G. sylvaticum* ssp. *rivulare* are long explosive 'crane's-bills'.

Common Dog Violet *Viola riviniana* VIOLACEAE
P.3–5. To 20cm. Widespread Europe, except S.E.
V. riviniana is a typical violet of springtime woods and hedgerows, sometimes abundant. Flower stalks and a central non-flowering cluster of stalked heart-shaped leaves grow from the same point at ground level. Scentless flowers are rich blue-purple with a whitish fringed throat marked with purple guide lines; the 5 petals are fairly broad, evenly sized and overlapping; the blunt notched spur is paler.

Two-flowered Violet *Viola biflora* VIOLACEAE
P.6–8. To 20cm. Much of Europe. Mountains. Not British.
Usually found in the light shade of thin woodland and in rock crevices, this gay little plant has heart-shaped leaves and 2 bright yellow flowers, one often opening before the other. The 5 petals are unequal; 2 point upwards, 2 sideways; the largest one points downwards and is prolonged into a nectar-containing spur. Dark markings at the centre of the flower guide insects seeking the nectar.

Common Wintergreen *Pyrola minor* PYROLACEAE
P.5–7. 10–20cm. Most of Europe, rare in S. Woods, moors.
The Wintergreens are a small but fascinating group, often hiding amongst moss and rocks in coniferous woods. This species has small rounded flowers, drooping on tiny stalks in a terminal raceme. 5 pink-flushed, white, incurved petals enclose the 10 stamens and short thick style with its 5-lobed stigma. A single flower stem emerges from a loose basal growth of rounded-oval, stalked, glossy leaves.

Lesser Butterfly-orchid *Platanthera bifolia* ORCHIDACEAE
P.5–7. 25–30cm. Most of Europe. Varied habitats, open woods.
This plant and its relative, *P. chlorantha*, are readily distinguished from other European Orchids by their graceful spikes of delicate, pale greenish white, long-spurred flowers. To separate one from the other is less easy: the 2 pollinia of this species, seen best with a hand lens at the flower's throat, are erect and parallel whereas those of *P. chlorantha* are curved, diverging at the base. Two short, broad, unspotted leaves clasp the lower stem.

Giant Bellflower *Campanula latifolia* CAMPANULACEAE
P.7–8. 60–120cm. Most of Europe. Woods, bushy places.
A 'Giant' indeed, this is one of the largest Bellflowers and a most spectacular woodland plant, on rich, usually damp, ground. The term *'latifolia'* refers to the long-stalked lower leaves, which are both broad and long (to 15cm). They gradually decrease in size up the stem, becoming sessile and merging into bracts subtending the large short-stalked flowers. These, in a long raceme, are a delightful pale blue, with 5 linear pointed sepals and 5 reflexed petal lobes.

Alpine Clematis *Clematis alpina* RANUNCULACEAE
P.6–7. 1–3.5m. Central Alps; 900–2300m. Not British.
Europe's only Alpine climbing plant provides a glorious picture when its large purple flowers festoon dark pine branches and cascade over steep rock faces. Delicately lobed leaves spread from slender stalks, which, wiry and sensitive, become next year's climbing agents. The flowers are readily identified by their 4 long purple sepals, spreading around a centre of numerous, strap-like, white staminodes, normal stamens and pistils; they are followed by equally beautiful plumed seed heads.

Ground-ivy *Glechoma hederacea* LABIATAE
P.3–5. 10–30cm. Most of Europe. Damp woods and grassland.
Although usually mat-forming, Ground-ivy sometimes provides a fascinating rock-garden picture around old tree stumps or on steep banks of woodland streams. Creeping stems produce erect flowering branches, softly hairy and with alternate pairs of stalked leaves, kidney-shaped and evenly crenate. In the axils grow whorls of 2–10 dark purple-blue flowers, each with a hairy tubular calyx and a longer bilabiate corolla. The upper lip is small, 2-lobed and erect; the larger lower one is deeply divided into 3 lobes and spotted with purple.

Stinking Iris *Iris foetidissima* IRIDACEAE
P.5–7. 30–90cm. S. and W. Europe. Woods, hedges, sea-cliffs.
The large strangely beautiful flowers of Irises are quite distinctive: 3 outer petals (falls) tend to droop; 3 inner ones (standards) are often erect around 3 stamens and a 3-lobed, sometimes leafy, style. Stems and leaves are glabrous and stiff; the leaves sharply edged and pointed, hence the alternative name of Gladdon—'swordlike'. When broken, they smell strongly of raw meat—hence another name, Roast-beef Plant. Pale purple flowers, though small, are tinged yellow with delicate darker veining. The distinguishing character of this species is the conspicuous brilliance of its red-orange seeds, vividly displayed in autumn as the large green pods split longitudinally into 3.

Creeping Lady's-tresses *Goodyera repens* ORCHIDACEAE
P.7–9. 10–25cm. Chiefly N. Widespread. Coniferous woods.
This small pale orchid with creeping rooting stems and erect, glandular, hairy flowering stems usually inhabits mossy pine woods. Its base is surrounded by a few broad leaves about 2cm long; smaller ones sheathe the stem, gradually reducing to bracts which subtend tiny fragrant white flowers. 12–25 flowers form a compact slightly twisted spike; the upper glandular petals make a hood above the short pouched lip.

One-flowered Wintergreen *Moneses uniflora* PYROLACEAE
P.6–8. 5–12cm. Widespread, local. Coniferous woods to 2100m.
This exquisite little plant of Arctic and Alpine woods grows around tree stumps and in shady mossy places. Stalked, shining, evergreen leaves, rounded and finely toothed, grow low on the single erect flowering stem, which carries 1 drooping fragrant flower. This is flat and creamy white with 5 small sepals and 5 large wavy-edged petals; 10 stamens are 2 to a petal, and the green pistil is prominent in the centre.

Serrated Wintergreen *Orthilia secunda* PYROLACEAE
P.7–8. 6–16cm. Most of Europe. Woods, moors.
Scattered colonies of this little plant nestle inconspicuously around mossy boulders and tree bases in coniferous woodlands. The stems, at first procumbent, become erect at flowering time, with several stalked, glossy evergreen leaves, oval-pointed, in irregular whorls. Above rises a terminal 1-sided raceme of about 10 small, nodding, pale green flowers, each with 5 petals curving around 10 crowded anthers; the style and 5-lobed stigma project well beyond them.

Greenish Wintergreen *Pyrola chlorantha* PYROLACEAE
P.6–7. 5–10cm. Much Europe, especially N. mountain woods.
This dainty Wintergreen of coniferous woodlands, almost lost amongst the vegetation, has short thin stems and small pale green flowers. The leaves are all basal, more round and less pointed than those of *Orthilia secunda*, finely dentate, on long stalks. Flowers are few, slightly drooping in a loose raceme, *not* 1-sided; they open fairly wide to display a long, curved, protruding style. Not British.

Twinflower *Linnaea borealis* CAPRIFOLIACEAE
P.7–8. 5–10cm. N. Europe; rare in Alps. 1200–2200m.
Though beautifully delicate, this plant, named for the botanist, Linnaeus, possesses tough trailing stems. These produce numerous leafy branches from which grow thin, erect, hairy flowering stems. 2 bell-like, 5-lobed flowers hang from the top of each stem, pale pink with darker lines and fragrant. The crowded small leaves are paired and almost round, slightly indented and darker above than beneath.

Chickweed Wintergreen *Trientalis europaea* PRIMULACEAE
P.6–7. 10–20cm. Much of Europe, chiefly N. Alps to 2000m.
Coniferous woods.
These slender plants of damp grassy or mossy places are unrelated to the previous Wintergreens. An erect stem ends with a whorl of about 6 bright green shiny leaves, of different sizes, entire, oval-linear and spreading; 1–2 very small ones may occur lower down. Above the whorl arises 1 starry white flower (occasionally more) with usually 7 narrow pinkish sepals, 7 broad overlapping petals and 7 stamens.

May Lily *Maianthemum bifolium* LILIACEAE
P.5–7. 8–15cm. Most of Europe. Humus-rich woods; local.
Sometimes abundant in moist places amongst conifers, May Lily is a most charming small woodland plant. From a creeping rhizome grow slender erect stems bearing 2 heart-shaped leaves, the lower one much larger than the upper (*c*. 6.5 and 3.5cm.). Above, the stem ends in a dainty raceme of tiny stalked white flowers, each with 4 spreading petals, 4 long stamens, and a small round ovary, later enlarging into a berry.

Lesser Bulrush *Typha angustifolia* TYPHACEAE
P.6–8. To 2m. Most of Europe. Aquatic; locally common.
From underwater mud, thick creeping rhizomes produce stiff erect stems with several pairs of long sheathing leaves, 1cm wide. Small female flowers pack the familiar brown spike, later fluffy with grey-haired seed heads, which is separated from the yellowish male-flowered inflorescence above by a gap of 1–9cm. The gap distinguishes it from *T. latifolia*, in which the 2 spikes are contiguous and the leaves 2.5cm wide.

Bogbean *Menyanthes trifoliata* MENYANTHACEAE
P.5–7. 10–30cm. Most of Europe. Ponds, lake margins, marshes; to 2400m.
Shallow open water in winter becomes a small forest of large 3-lobed leaves from spring to autumn, enhanced in summer by the glorious mingling of pink buds and white flowers of Bogbean. Flowers and leaves grow separately from strong mud-based rhizomes. The bell-shaped, 5-petalled flowers remain pink-flushed outside and white inside, beautifully fringed with wavy white hairs.

White Water-lily *Nymphaea alba* NYMPHAEACEAE
P.6–9. To 3m. Most of Europe. Aquatic; to depths of 2m.
In calm waters, the long, spongy, flexible stalks of the White Water-lily, adaptable to varying water levels, arise from stout mud-rooted rhizomes; so do long-stalked flat glossy leaves, 10–30cm across, deeply indented basally. Each flower has about 20 spirally arranged petals, becoming smaller from the outer ring inwards, finally grading into golden-anthered stamens, encircling the yellow-rayed stigma.

Water Lobelia *Lobelia dortmanna* LOBELIACEAE
P.6–8. 20–40cm. Chiefly W. and N. Europe. Aquatic.
This peculiar, apparently delicate plant is visible for only a few weeks, when slender, leafless stems appear above water around shallow gravelly margins of mountain lakes. A few scattered pale lilac flowers droop from short stalks, each corolla a slit tube with 5 irregular spreading lobes. Permanently submerged are tufts of short bright green leaves, each a double-hollowed tube, giving great strength and resilience.

Fringed Water-lily *Nymphoides peltata* MENYANTHACEAE
P.6–9. Much of Europe. Aquatic; locally common.
This beautiful plant of calm waters, related to Bogbean, is of Water-lily habit. Long-stalked leaves and flowering stems grow from mud-based rhizomes and small, glossy, round leaves float on the water, the funnel-shaped flowers held above. Bright golden yellow, about 5cm diameter, the 5 spreading petal lobes are wide and overlapping, with finely fringed margins. The 5 stamens and stigma are also yellow.

Frogbit *Hydrocharis morsus-ranae* HYDROCHARITACEAE
P.7–8. Most of Europe, rare Mediterranean. Aquatic; still water.
Frogbit is free-floating, sometimes in thick mats; long horizontal underwater stems produce plants at intervals, whose roots absorb nutriment directly from the water. Numerous round leaves float in rosettes around a few unisexual white flowers with 3 delicate crinkled petals, blotched yellow at the base. In autumn, the stems produce overwintering buds. These settle on the mud, rising again to start new growth next spring.

Lesser Water-plantain *Baldellia ranunculoides* ALISMATACEAE
P.5–8. 5–20cm. S., W. and C. Europe. Watersides, fens.
Related to the tall Water-plantains of ponds, ditches and lake margins, this smaller plant usually grows in wet mud around such waters. Erect, spreading or even decumbent, it roots and produces small tufted plants at intervals. The linear leaves' short pointed blades narrow gradually into long stalks; flowers are comparatively large, on unequal stalks and with 3 lilac-purple petals.

Yellow Iris *Iris pseudacorus* IRIDACEAE
P. 5–7. 40–100cm. Most of Europe. Pond, lake, river margins.
Widespread and conspicuous, Europe's commonest Iris forms sheets of gold by streams, lakes, ponds and in marshland. Stiff, erect, glaucous stems and leaves are of similar height, the former with a few flowering side branches. A few showy flowers, at first enfolded by 2 papery bracts, bloom in sequence; their 'falls' are large, deflexed, often purple-veined; the 'standards' are small, narrow and upright.

Branched Bur-reed *Sparganium erectum* SPARGANIACEAE
P.6–8. 0.5–2m. All Europe. Shallow water, muddy lake margins.
The shining stems and keeled leaves of Bur-reed are found in and beside slow-flowing water. The leaves overtop the inflorescences, spiky balls on short side branches. Above are male flowers, yellow with pollen when mature; females are green except for protruding white styles and stigmas. After pollination, the males soon fade but the females develop into seeds (burs), which float on the water for dispersal.

Water-soldier *Stratiotes aloides* HYDROCHARITACEAE
P.6–8. 5–20cm. Much of Europe. Aquatic, free floating. Local.
For most of the year this plant is unseen, then suddenly the water surface is broken by circles of sharp green points. These rise until the pond is choked with an 'army' of fierce saw-edged leaves, each circle guarding 1 or a few glorious white, 3-petalled, unisexual flowers. Flowering time over, the 'army' sinks to rest again on the underwater mud.

Arrowhead *Sagittaria sagittifolia* ALISMATACEAE
P.7–9. 30–90cm. Most of Europe. Aquatic, still and slow water.
Arrowhead's large aerial leaves are unmistakable; sharply divided into 3 typically arrow-shaped points, they grow singly on long flexible stalks. When present, underwater or floating leaves are simple in outline. Also aerial, on leafless stems, attractive flowers grow in whorls, usually 3 together; their 3 wide white petals are beautifully splashed with purple. Uppermost, staminate flowers display numerous purple anthers and golden pollen and, below, rounded hard seed heads follow the female flowers.

Flowering-rush *Butomus umbellatus* BUTOMACEAE
P.7–9. To 1.5m. Most of Europe. Shallow water, margins, local.
The flowering-rush is a most spectacularly beautiful waterside plant. Surrounded by numerous, long, narrow, sharp-edged leaves, each stem produces a spreading cluster of some 20 large flowers on stalks of varying lengths. They show all flowering stages, from buds to seed heads and are all shades of pink. Stamens with red anthers ripen before the red carpels (both 6–9); seeds are dispersed by water.

Wild Angelica *Angelica sylvestris* UMBELLIFERAE
P.7–9. 30–200cm. Most of Europe. Streamsides, damp, shade.
This attractive species displays large frothy pinkish cream flower heads amongst the brighter colours of other waterside plants. Numerous small flowers constitute the rounded umbels, which grow terminally and in leaf axils. The upper leaves are almost reduced to pale green sheaths, contrasting with the large, serrate, long-stalked, lower leaves, up to 60cm across and 2 or 3 times pinnately divided.

Brooklime *Veronica beccabunga* S-ROPHULARIACEAE
P.5–9. 20–60cm. All Europe. Streams, ditches, marshes.
The typical flowers of this *Veronica* tend to be overshadowed by the numerous glossy crenate leaves. These grow in pairs on smooth fleshy stems, which at first creep through the mud and produce roots and aerial branches at intervals; later they become erect. The small vivid blue flowers, in long-stalked axillary clusters, are white-centred, with 2 stamens and 4 unequal outspread petals.

Goat Willow *Salix caprea* SALICACEAE
P.3–4. 3–10m. Most of Europe. Banks of rivers; scrub.
Often called Pussy Willow because of its furry catkins, this small tree is one of the joys of spring. Its furrowed grey trunk breaks into numerous spreading branches, covered with catkins—petal-less flowers—before the oval leaves appear. The trees are dioecious, the female catkins crowded with green pistils, later fluffy with seed, while the silver fur of the male flowers is followed by a burst of golden anthers.

Purple-loosestrife *Lythrum salicaria* LYTHRACEAE
P.6–8. 60–120cm. Most of Europe. Fens, riversides, damp areas.
A most richly colourful waterside plant, Purple-loosestrife has distinctive masses of long rosy purple plumes of whorled flowers. Square branching stems are purple-tinged and thick with long, rather narrow, pointed leaves. 3 forms of flowers are produced on different plants; all have 5 or 6 separate, narrow, somewhat crinkled petals; lengths of the 12 stamens and style vary to assist cross pollination.

Royal-fern *Osmunda regalis* OSMUNDACEAE
P.6–8. To 4m. W. Europe, rarer E.; local. Damp places.
Truly regal amongst ferns, this large, tufted plant grows from erect thick mud-based rhizomes. The large leaf-like fronds are twice pinnate, the final divisions being from 0.5–4cm long and finely crenate. Ferns possess no true flowers or seeds but produce asexual spores, usually on the underside of the fronds but, in this plant, in dense tawny masses on long terminal branches, erect amidst and above the numerous fronds.

St Patrick's-cabbage *Saxifrage spathularis* SAXIFRAGACEAE
P.5–8. 20–30cm. N. Portugal, N.W. Spain, Ireland. Endemic.

Starry Saxifrage *Saxifraga stellaris* SAXIFRAGACEAE
P.6–8. 4–20cm. Arctic-alpine; widespread. Streamsides, bogs.

Yellow Saxifrage *Saxifraga aizoides* SAXIFRAGACEAE
P.6–8. To 25cm. Arctic-alpine; locally abundant.
Saxifrages belong primarily, although not exclusively, to the mountains of the world. In Europe about 120 species are recorded, in varying situations and at almost all heights, from dry rocks to sodden bogland. Many are low-growing because of the fierce climatic conditions, with leaves variously adapted to reduce water loss. Flowers are 5-petalled 'stars', usually in clusters, and, in the 'cushion' types especially, they frequently cover the whole plant. Although some species are difficult to identify, the genus is distinctive.
S. spathularis is a local species on wet, acid, mountain rocks (sea cliffs in Ireland) with a basal rosette of shining, crenate, spoon-shaped leaves, shorter than their stalks. Small, pinkish white, spotted flowers grow in clusters, branching from a leafless hairy stem.
S. stellaris is common in mountain bogs and streams, superficially like *S. spathularis* but smaller. Leaves grow in basal rosettes but are sessile, longer than wide and sparsely dentate. Flowers are small, white, with yellow spots.
S. aizoides forms gold and green cascades by mountain streams and waterfalls. Small linear leaves are glossy; the yellow flowers have narrow petals spotted orange or red; sometimes red flowers are found.

Marsh-marigold *Caltha palustris* RANUNCULACEAE
P.3–5. To 30cm. Most of Europe. Streamsides, wet meadows.
The large brilliant flowers give Marsh-marigold many popular names and transform wintery wetness into a golden carpet. Branching stems and leaves are glossy; lower leaves large, long-stalked, deeply lobed at the base, the upper ones sessile and small. Flowers are saucer-shaped without sepals but with 5–8 shining petals, rounded and overlapping. Numerous, spirally arranged stamens surround a few green carpels which later enlarge into hard seed heads.

Common Fritillary *Fritillaria meleagris* LILIACEAE
P.4–5. 25–45cm. C. Europe, N. to S. England. Endemic.
Water meadows, periodically submerged by overflowing rivers before flowering time, were once patterned pink with the beautiful nodding flowers of Common Fritillaries; sadly they are now rare, due largely to farming changes. This bulbous plant has a single stem, a few greyish grass-like leaves and usually solitary flowers, chequerboard pink, occasionally white, bell-shaped with 6 overlapping bluntly pointed petals.

Loose-flowered Orchid *Orchis laxiflora* ORCHIDACEAE
P.5–6. 30–75cm. W. and S. Europe; Channel Isles. Not common.
These tall strong orchids, whose long loose spikes of rich purple flowers may be abundant locally, grow in water-soaked meadows. Narrow, keeled, unspotted leaves sheathe the stem alternately. Above them, purplish bracts subtend the typical *Orchid* flowers, with 2 outer, erect, reflexed petal segments, a shorter hood formed by 3 inner ones and a 3-lobed lip (the central lobe very small), whose centre is white or nearly so.

Ragged-Robin *Lychnis flos-cuculi* CARYOPHYLLACEAE
P.5–6. 30–80cm. Most of Europe. Damp meadows, marshes.
Related to Red Campion (p. 60), Ragged-Robin flaunts masses of rosy pink shagginess, sometimes abundantly. The stems are erect, slender, somewhat rough, with short stiff hairs, red at the base and with opposite pairs of simple leaves. Flowers grow in loose, branched, terminal clusters; above a slightly inflated ridged calyx are 5 spreading petals, deeply cut into 4, narrow, unequal lobes with 10 stamens in the throat.

Marsh Woundwort *Stachys palustris* LABIATAE
P.7–9. 40–100cm. Most of Europe. Streamsides, damp places.
The pale purple spikes of Marsh Woundwort mingle with the similarly coloured Water Mint by rivers and lakes in late summer. Erect, slightly branched, angular stems carry numerous pairs of sessile or short-stalked simple leaves, from 5–12cm long, softly hairy and finely toothed. In the upper axils, bilabiate flowers grow in whorls; upper petals small and hooded, the lip spreading, lobed and patterned white on purple.

Bird's-eye Primrose *Primula farinosa* PRIMULACEAE
P.5–7. 3–15cm. Much of Europe. Chiefly mountains. Local.
This is a charming little plant, whether suffusing lime-based peaty marshland with soft pinkish lilac or contrasting with vivid blue gentians in damp mountain pastures. From ground rosettes of small, finely toothed, spathulate leaves, green above, thickly mealy beneath, grow slender stems bearing rounded clusters of delicate flowers, occasionally white, on very short stalks. These are typically either 'pin'-eyed or 'thrum'-eyed, yellow-centred, with 5, deeply notched, separate petals.

Bog Pimpernel *Anagallis tenella* PRIMULACEAE
P.5–8. 5–15cm. Mainly W. Europe. Peat bogs, ditches, slacks.
This, perhaps the most delicately lovely bog plant, has fine stems which thread through the wet surface of sphagnum or peat. Short roots sprout from the stems, which also produce a carpet of small, rounded, almost sessile leaves, thus establishing the plant's territory against strong competition. From the leaf axils grow thin, erect, flower stalks, carrying single shell-pink flowers.

Fen Violet *Viola persicifolia* VIOLACEAE
P.5–6. 8–20cm. Most of Europe. Marshes, fens.
Heart-shaped leaves are characteristic of most violets but those of this species are twice as long as broad, with an almost straight base, long-stalked and crenate with leafy stipules. Slender stalks, up to 6cm long, carry solitary pale lilac (occasionally white) flowers, each with 5 short sepals with backward-pointing lobes, 5 rounded overlapping petals and a blunt greenish spur. There is no central non-flowering rosette.

Marsh Cinquefoil *Potentilla palustris* ROSACEAE
P.6–7. 15–45cm. Most of Europe, not extreme S. Marshes, fens.
These beautifully unusual wine-red flowers are not always immediately discernible amongst taller, thick, waterside vegetation, but are easily recognised. They grow in loose clusters from the axils of stalked, usually 5-lobed leaves, (sometimes 3 or 7), dark green above, greyish below and sharply toothed. Each flower has 5 tiny outer sepals, 5 large inner ones resembling petals and 5 small true petals. All are dark soft red and pointed, surrounding numerous darker stamens and pistils.

Water Avens *Geum rivale* ROSACEAE
P.5–7. 20–60cm. Most of Europe. Streamsides, wet meadows.
The unusual colours of Water Avens display a fascinating theme, from erect maroon stems to nodding bi-coloured flowers. A double calyx of pointed, wine-red sepals closely surrounds 5 alternating petals, rounded, notched and yellowish pink with darker pink veining. Packed within this double cup are numerous yellow-anthered stamens and feathery hooked styles, which lengthen into round heads of bristly brown seeds.

Cuckooflower *Cardamine pratensis* CRUCIFERAE
P. 4–6. 20–60cm. Widespread Europe. Damp fields, streamsides.
The delicately flowered Lady's-smock (its second name) is frequently found in abundance, together with sharply contrasting, brilliant Marsh-marigolds. A basal rosette of long-stalked pinnate leaves, with rounded, sparsely toothed lobes, surrounds the erect stem, whose leaves become progressively smaller with narrowing lobes. The stalked 4-petalled flowers form a short terminal cluster and vary from white through all shades of lilac-purple around 6 central golden stamens (4 long, 2 short).

Grass-of-Parnassus *Parnassia palustris* PARNASSIACEAE
P.7–10. 10–30cm. Most Europe; local. Marshy land, dune slacks.
These exquisite plants are more akin to Saxifrages than Grasses. Each produces several separate, long-stalked, heart-shaped leaves and taller flowering stems with 1 leaf near the base. Young flowers are cup-shaped, becoming almost flat when mature, with 5 large, green-veined, white petals. 5 normal stamens alternate with 5 glandular-fringed staminodes which produce nectar.

Gorse *Ulex europaeus* LEGUMINOSAE
P.(1)–2–6–(12). 60–200cm. W. Europe to Italy. Heath.

Western Gorse *Ulex gallii* LEGUMINOSAE
P.7–10. 30–90cm. More extreme W. Europe. Heathland.
The European species of Gorse are stiff, much-branched, very spiny shrubs easily recognised as a group, but with small specific variations, sometimes requiring a lens to distinguish them. Their dark green ridged stems are crowded with short spiny branches bearing small linear leaves, also ending in sharp prickles. By contrast, their massed golden butterfly flowers provide a glorious display of brilliant colour for much of the year, to be followed by dry seed pods which burst with explosive 'pops'.
U. europaeus, with sweetly scented flowers, is the largest and most widespread species, well-known for its almost year-long flowering.
U. gallii is restricted to the more extreme west, from Scotland to N.W. Spain, and is shorter with smaller flowers. Its stem hairs are pale brown and abundant, whereas those of *U. europaeus* are black and sparse.

Dodder *Cuscuta epithymum* CONVOLVULACEAE
A.6–10. Most of Europe except far N. Heathland.
When familiar Gorse and Heather shrubs appear enmeshed in a tangle of fine red threads, the parasitic Dodder has established its hold. Aerial for most of its life, Dodder obtains all its nutriment from the host plant, by absorption through red suckers on the probing sensitive stems, after becoming attached to the host. The leaves are tiny scales and the massed clusters of pink waxen flowers are surprisingly pretty.

Marsh Arrowgrass *Triglochin palustris* JUNCAGINACEAE
P.6–8. 15–40cm. Most of Europe. Marshes, wet meadows.
These grass-like plants are undistinguished especially in amongst tall grasses. Several narrow grooved leaves grow from sheathing bases and surround a single, longer, unbranched flowering stem. The small inconspicuous flowers, in a long raceme, are predominantly green with 6 purple-tipped petals, yellow stamens, and tufty white stigmas. Seed capsules are long, green and shining.

Yellow Bartsia *Parentucellia viscosa* SCROPHULARIACEAE
A.6–10. 10–15cm. S. and W. Europe. Damp grassy places.
Stems, leaves and calyx of *Parentucellia* are all extremely sticky, due to a thick covering of beautiful, reddish, shining glandular hairs. Tall leafy stems end in a long spike of flowers in the upper leaf axils; all leaves are simple and toothed. The tubular calyx spreads into 4 long lobes around the bilabiate corolla. The upper lip is short and paler than the lower bright yellow lip with 3 rounded lobes.

Globeflower *Trollius europaeus* RANUNCULACEAE
P.5–7. 10–50cm. Most of Europe, especially mts. To 2800m.
From moist upland meadows to wet mountain ledges, the leafy plants and glorious golden heads of Globeflowers are always a joyous discovery. Leaves are palmately lobed, the lobes further divided and toothed. Flowers consist of 5–15 large yellow sepals, overlapping into an almost closed ball hiding the same number of small nectaries and numerous stamens and carpels. Only tiny creeping insects can therefore reach the nectar and effect cross-pollination.

Long-leaved Butterwort *Pinguicula longifolia*
LENTIBULARIACEAE
P.6. 5–15cm. Mountains of S. Europe. To 1600m. Not British.

Alpine Butterwort *Pinguicula alpina* LENTIBULARIACEAE
P.5–8. 5–10cm. Arctic-alpine Europe. To 2600m. Not British.

Butterwort *Pinguicula leptoceras* LENTIBULARIACEAE
P.5–7. 5–15cm. Most European mts. To 2500m. Not British.
Butterworts are distinctively unique in appearance. On wet grassland, soggy peat and watery cliff ledges, they spread flat rosettes of simple yellow-green leaves with inrolled margins. These leaves, shining and greasy, attract and hold small insects; numerous tiny glands cover their surface and pour out digestive juices which absorb the insects' soft parts, supplementing an otherwise inadequate diet. The large attractive flowers are solitary and almost horizontal on long slender stalks arising directly from the shallow-based root stock. Each has 2 lips; the upper 2-lobed, the lower larger and 3-lobed; a spur projects backwards.
P. longifolia, the rarest of these 3, prefers wet rocks and has very yellowish, narrow, wavy-edged leaves, 6–13cm long, large mid-violet flowers with lobes of the lower lip not overlapping and a thin curved spur.
P. alpina is the most widespread and common species shown and the only white-flowered one; the flowers are rather small with a bright yellow centre and a short conical spur.
P. leptoceras is similar to the most common species, *P. vulgaris* (which is British), but its dark purple flowers are broader with a large, white, very hairy central patch. Rare.

Summer Snowflake *Leucojum aestivum* AMARYLLIDACEAE
P.4–6. 30–60cm. Chiefly C. and S. Europe; often naturalised.
Before the main flush of riverside vegetation, the clear white flowers of these graceful plants droop from tall 3-angled stems, mingled with often longer keeled shining leaves. A single sheathing bract subtends 2–7 flowers, whose slender arching stalks vary in length, the topmost being longest with the first-opened flower. 6 separate equal petals form a bell-shaped corolla, splashed with green just above each slightly reflexed tip.

Marsh-orchid *Dactylorhiza majalis* ORCHIDACEAE
P.5–7. 20–60cm. W., C. Europe. Marshes, wet meadows.

Common Spotted-orchid *D. fuchsii* ORCHIDACEAE
P.6–8. 15–60cm. Most of Europe. Damp grassland; widespread.

Southern Marsh-orchid *D. m.* ssp. *praetermissa* ORCHIDACEAE
P.6–7. 15–60cm. N.W. Europe. Endemic. Damp meadows, fens.

Northern Marsh-orchid *D. m.* ssp. *purpurella* ORCHIDACEAE
P.6–8. 20–45cm. N.W. Europe. Endemic. Damp meadows.

These typical wild orchids of Europe are found in wet places, especially grassland and fens, often preferring base-rich soils. Locally abundant, they seem to belie the 'Orchids are rare, don't touch' appeal, but that abundance *is* only local and not necessarily permanent.

Dactylorhiza was separated from the similar genus, *Orchis*, because of certain stable differences, notably in the structure of the underground tubers. Those of *Orchis* are egg-shaped whereas those of *Dactylorhiza* are 5-lobed or divided ('*dactyl*' is from the Greek word for finger).

Typical inflorescences are densely flowered with leafy bracts; petals are erect or spreading, but not forming a hood as in *Orchis*, and are of varying rich shades of purple, except for a few yellow continental species.

Within the genus, naming is controversial and difficult because the species are variable in details and freely hybridise. Our names are taken from *Flora Europaea* (1980), Vol. 5; older books give full specific rank to *D. praetermissa* and *D. purpurella*.

D. majalis; leaves broad, widest at or below the middle, heavily purple-spotted. Flowers usually rich purple, with central markings. Not British but has close relative in Ireland and Wales. Grows to 2500m.

D. fuchsii; leaves fairly broad, spotted; flowers mauve to pinkish with red-purple spots and lines, occasionally white; lip deeply 3-lobed.

D. m. ssp. *praetermissa*; leaves light green, unspotted, widest below middle. Flowers pinkish to rosy purple, lip shallowly 3-lobed, mid-lobe speckled red.

D. m. ssp. *purpurella*; leaves somewhat blue-green, usually unspotted; flowers deep magenta-purple, lip scarcely lobed with dark markings.

Bog bilberry *Vaccinium uliginosum* ERICACEAE
P.5–6. 30–50cm. N. and C. Europe. Moors; mts to 3100m.

Cowberry *Vaccinium vitis-idaea* ERICACEAE
P.5–8. 10–30cm. Most of Europe. Coniferous woods, moors, mts.

Bilberry *Vaccinium myrtillus* ERICACEAE
P. 5–7. 20–60cm. Most of Europe. Heaths, moors, mts to 2800 m.

This primarily moorland, mountain and arctic genus includes several plants which are widespread and frequently dominant over wide areas. They are dwarf shrubs, able to withstand bleak windswept terrain, a difficult climate and poor, usually acid soil because they are slow-growing, with strong creeping rhizomes, tough stems and leaves adapted to prevent excessive transpiration. Many are evergreen, thickly covered with glossy leaves, sometimes hairy beneath, with inrolled margins. At flowering time, pale waxen blossoms mingle with the shining leaves.

V. uliginosum is deciduous with rather thin, bluish green, strongly veined leaves. Small, creamy pink, campanulate flowers with tiny reflexed lobes droop from the upper leaf axils. Berries are large, black, glaucous, sweet and reputed edible in small quantities.

V. vitis-idaea has leathery evergreen leaves, glossy above, paler with brown glands below and with slightly inrolled margins. The white, pink-tinged flowers, wide at the throat, droop in terminal racemes. Berries are globular, bright red and edible.

V. myrtillus produces large glaucous blue berries, delicious in pies and jam. Plants are deciduous with bright green, finely toothed leaves and pink globular flowers, constricted at the throat.

Round-leaved Wintergreen *Pyrola rotundifolia* PYROLACEAE
P.6–9. 10–20cm. Most of Europe, especially N. and mountains.
Larger and more conspicuous than the 4 woodland Wintergreens (p. 80),
this plant also favours coniferous woods, but prefers wet places; a slightly
different form is sometimes abundant in sand-dune slacks. The round,
glossy, stalked leaves and terminal raceme of drooping flowers follow the
Pyrola pattern, but the flowers are wide, almost flat, with 5, rounded,
overlapping white petals. The projecting style is longer than in other
species and is markedly curved.

Bog Rosemary *Andromeda polifolia* ERICACEAE
P.5–6. To 25cm. C. and N. Europe to Arctic coast. Peat bogs.
The exquisite rose pink flowers of Bog Rosemary grace the wetter parts of
northern peat bogs. A creeping root stock produces erect, tough, leafy
stems; the leaves are evergreen, linear, to 3cm long, dark green and
reticulate above, grey below, with inrolled margins and sharply pointed
tips. Above them, a few clustered flowers droop on short pink stalks,
delicate and rounded with 5 reflexed lobes around a very narrow throat.

Yellow Centaury *Cicendia filiformis* GENTIANACEAE
A.6–9. 2–12cm. S. and W. Europe. Not far from the sea.
These strange little plants are so tiny that they are easily overlooked in
their natural home of moist sandy or peaty ground. The leaves, from
2–6mm long, are few, sessile, linear, growing in pairs at the base and along
the fine, slender, slightly branched stems. Each branch ends in a solitary
flower like a yellow pinhead, until the 4 petal lobes unfold, which they do
only in warm bright sunshine.

Bog Asphodel *Narthecium ossifragum* LILIACEAE
P.7–8. 10–30cm. N. and W. Europe. Acid bogs, wet heaths.
One of the most glorious displays of wet peaty moorland is that of the
vivid Bog Asphodel, whose star-like flowers are locally abundant. Each
stiffly erect stem is surrounded by shorter sword-like leaves, and carries a
tight raceme of golden flowers, each with 6 outspread narrow petals and 6
stamens with beautifully furry filaments. After flowering, the whole plant
darkens to a rich tawny colour, persistent throughout autumn.

Broom *Cytisus scoparius* LEGUMINOSAE
P.4–6. 60–200cm. Most of Europe, except extreme N. and E.
Superficially Broom resembles Gorse (p. 90) but without spines. This
species is widespread on sandy heaths and waste ground; although native,
it is also planted and naturalised. The shrubby plant has smooth green
branches and small stalked leaves, mostly trifoliate. The bright yellow
flowers are similar to those of Gorse but with smaller hairless sepals; seed
pods are black with hairy margins. The branches were used for brooms.

Cloudberry *Rubus chamaemorus* ROSACEAE
P.6–8. 5–20cm. Mostly N. Europe. Moors, bogs, to 1400m.
Cloudberry is a low-growing non-prickly relative of the hedgerow
Brambles, locally abundant, especially in Arctic bogland. Its reddish
stems carry large leaves, palmately lobed, finely toothed and beautifully
reticulate above. Solitary, pure white flowers are monoecious with 5
broad petals and 5 smaller pointed sepals which become dark red after
flowering. They are then reflexed below the soft edible fruit, which
changes from red to orange when ripe.

Bog Orchid *Hammarbya paludosa* ORCHIDACEAE
P.7–9. 5–12cm. N. and C. Europe, E. to Russia. Acid bogs.
This thin green orchid grows half buried in the soggiest of wet Sphagnum
bogs, and possesses some unusual features. Wrapped in sheathing basal
leaves are 2 pseudobulbs (stem swellings) for food storage, one above the
other. Tiny buds around the tips of the stem leaves drop away to form new
plants; the flower lip stands erect due to a full circle twisting of the ovary.
'*Hammarbya*' commemorates the home of Swedish botanist, Linnaeus.

Marsh Gentian *Gentiana pneumonanthe* GENTIANACEAE
P.7–10. 15–30cm. Most of Europe. Wet heaths, bogs; local.
The rare Marsh Gentian possesses an ethereal beauty of its own, which is enhanced by its contrasting peaty boggy habitat. Single, slender, unbranched stems are clothed with narrow paired leaves to 2.5cm long; above rises a cluster of 1–6 funnel-shaped flowers of a soft almost translucent blue (rarely white). Spirally coiled in bud, lightly spotted and streaked with pale green, the 5 short petal lobes unfold to spread horizontally outwards—but only when the sun is shining!

Heather *Calluna vulgaris* ERICACEAE
P.7–9. To 60cm. Most of Europe. Heaths, moors.
Heather brings a warm welcome glow to miles of moorland when summer is nearly over. Tough and woody, the branching twigs are thickly clothed with tiny evergreen leaves (1–2mm long) and small flowers. The former are sessile in short, close-packed rows and the latter are crowded in narrow, terminal racemes. Their light purple colour is provided by both sepals and petals (4 each) forming an open corolla, different from the frequently drooping, narrow-throated flowers of *Erica*.

Bog Myrtle *Myrica gale* MYRICACEAE
P.4–5. To 2.5m. W. and N.W. Europe. Bogs and heaths.
Considerable areas of wet moorland are sometimes dominated by this deciduous, densely branched shrub whose grey-green leaves scent the air in summer-time. Both surfaces of the leaves possess small yellow resinous glands, the origin of this delightful fragrance. The leaves follow the early flowering of inconspicuous catkins; the plants are usually dioecious, though not always so. The tiny flowers have neither sepals nor petals; the male catkins consist of brown overlapping scales, each sheltering 6–8 stamens with red anthers, and the females have 2 small ovaries topped by 2 red stigmas. Short spikes of hard green seeds develop later. The leaves have been much used for home brewing of Gale beer.

Bell Heather *Erica cinerea* ERICACEAE
P.7–9. To 60cm. N. and W. Europe. Heaths, moors, cliffs.

Dorset Heath *Erica ciliaris* ERICACEAE
P.6–9. 15–45cm. Extreme W. Europe. Heaths, bogs.
These two representatives of *Erica*, commonly called Heaths, are good examples of the European members of this colourfully attractive genus. All are evergreen, branching shrubs with small linear leaves and spikes of rich purple or pink (rarely white), tubular, urn-shaped flowers. They are distinguished from *Calluna* by the flower shape, non-petaloid calyx and whorled arrangement of the usually longer leaves.
E. cinerea is widespread and locally abundant, with long cylindrical flower spikes (to 15cm). The flowers droop in rather loose whorls, transforming the moorland scene into a glowing carpet of glorious crimson-purple. The fine leaves are in whorls of 3, dark green with revolute margins.
E. ciliaris is locally plentiful, but of restricted distribution. The long dense flower spikes (5–12cm) are unilateral and tapering, with almost horizontal flowers of a deep rosy-pink. Leaves are in threes, very small, bright green above, greyish below with recurved margins thick with silvery glandular hairs.

St. Dabeoc's heath *Daboecia cantabrica* ERICACEAE
P.6–9. To 30cm. S.W. Europe. Endemic. Damp acid moors.
Daboecia, a beautiful but uncommon Heath, is locally dominant, displaying large, glowing, rose-purple flowers above leafy branching hairy twigs. The evergreen leaves are small (1cm long) and narrow with revolute margins, glossy green above, white with hairs below. The flowers droop in loose racemes; each urn-shaped corolla ends in 4 reflexed lobes, inside which are 4 almost black anthers; a maroon style and stigma project slightly when mature.

Lesser Twayblade *Listera cordata* ORCHIDACEAE
P.6–9. 6–20cm. Much of Europe. Wet moors; damp woods.
One of the least exotic Orchids, and easily missed in its boggy haunts, is this small delicate-looking plant with flowers of muted colours. Hidden beneath Heather or tucked in amongst wet mosses, the thin pinkish stems possess 1 pair of broad, pointed leaves, to 2.5cm long, slightly below the middle. The tiny pink and green flowers, about 6–12, form a short terminal raceme; each flower with 5 spreading petals and a distinctive hanging lip divided into 2 long segments.

Pitcherplant *Sarracenia purpurea* SARRACENIACEAE
P.5–7. 20–40cm. Introduced Europe from N. America. Peat bogs.
These extraordinary insectivorous plants were brought to Europe in about 1906 and are still found naturalised in W. Switzerland and C. Ireland, where they are well established in the wettest parts of very wet bogs. Their peculiar pitcher-like leaves, beautifully mottled yellow, green and purple-red, trap and absorb insects in the water collected in them. Each long stem ends in one large flower, also green and purple-red, in whose centre is an unusual stigma resembling an open green umbrella.

Round-leaved Sundew *Drosera rotundifolia* DROSERACEAE
P.6–8. 6–25cm. All Europe, not Mediterranean. Sphagnum bog.

Great Sundew *Drosera anglica* DROSERACEAE
P.7–8. 10–30cm. N. and C. Europe; rare S. Sphagnum bogs.

Oblong-leaved Sundew *Drosera intermedia* DROSERACEAE
P.6–8. 5–10cm. N., W. and C. Europe. Sphagnum bogs.
The Sundews are aptly named; their peculiar leaves are fringed with long-stalked glands, whose pinheads glisten and sparkle in bright sunlight. These exude a sticky fluid to attract small insects which, once caught, cannot escape. They are immediately held fast by the nearest tentacles bending over them and are digested by a juice poured over them by another set of glands.
Living always in very acid bogs, the plants' normal food supply is deficient, especially in nitrogen, and, by the evolution of this clever insectivorous mechanism, their needs are satisfied. The leaves grow in a long-stalked basal rosette, from the centre of which arise 1 or 2 slender flowering stems with a loose arching spike of tiny white flowers.
D. rotundifolia is the most common species with distinctly round leaves, usually spreading flat on the ground.
D. anglica is the largest; the leaves are long (3cm) and rather narrow, tapering gradually into long stalks, and almost erect, never on the ground.
D. intermedia, the smallest, has oval to narrow tapering leaves, only about 1cm long, with slightly longer stalks, spreading to nearly erect.

Dwarf Cornel *Cornus suecica* CORNACEAE
P.6–8. 10–15cm. N. Europe. Damp mountain moors to 1200m.
This delightful little plant contrasts sharply with the surrounding vegetation's special modifications for life in acid bogs. On slender stems grow several pairs of comparatively large, fresh green, soft leaves, entire, oval-pointed and with well marked veins. The flowers are very small, in a tight inky blue cluster, surrounded by 4 conspicuous wide white petal-like bracts. Later, the brilliant red berries are dispersed by birds.

Lesser Bladderwort *Utricularia minor* LENTIBULARIACEAE
P.6–9. 7–25cm. Most of Europe. Aquatic in shallow peaty pools.
Bladderworts are insectivorous like the Sundews but, as they are completely submerged for most of the year, finding and identifying them is not easy. This is the smallest; its 2–6 pale yellow flowers, on a slender, leafless stalk, appear above water in summertime. Tiny water insects are attracted into small, green, water-filled bladders attached to submerged thread-like leaves; the exit is blocked by a valve and the prey digested within the bladder.

Broom *Cytisus sessilifolius* LEGUMINOSAE
P.4–6. 1–2m. E. Spain, S. France, Italy. Not British.
Amongst the multifarious species of Broom adorning the dry sunny hills of southern Europe, this one is recognised by its fresh green, sessile leaves, whose 3, oval, pointed leaflets closely surround the main flowering stems. The leaves of non-flowering branches are long-stalked, trifoliate and smooth. Clear yellow 'butterfly' flowers grow in short terminal clusters; the shrubs are hairless and without spines.

Mouse-ear Hawkweed *Hieracium pilosella* COMPOSITAE
P.5–8. 5–30cm. Most of Europe. Dry grassy places.
The hundreds of species of bright-yellow-flowered composites, including Hawkweeds and Hawkbits, are extremely difficult to distinguish. This one, common in dry places, especially chalk downland, is relatively short-growing; characteristically pale yellow inflorescences have individual florets, striped red on the underside. This is a hairy plant with ground rosettes of 'mouse-ear' leaves, oval-oblong, furry-felted beneath and green with scattered hairs above.

Dark Mullein *Verbascum nigrum* SCROPHULARIACEAE
B or P.6–9. 50–120cm. Most of Europe. Grassy places.
Smaller than *V. thapsus*, this plant is more frequently found in roadside colonies. The somewhat downy hairs never mask the overall green colour of leaves and stem. Leaves are finely crenate-dentate and rather crinkled, the basal and lower ones stalked, the upper nearly sessile. Clusters of clear yellow flowers open in succession to give a long flowering season; the filament hairs are contrastingly rich purple.

Great Mullein *Verbascum thapsus* SCROPHULARIACEAE
B.6–9. 60–200cm. Most of Europe. Dry waste ground.
Also called Aaron's-rod, this distinctive Mullein has a usually unbranched, stiffly upright stem, very leafy below with a long crowded inflorescence above. It is densely woolly and greyish white with hairs, except for the large, flat, yellow flowers, opening erratically along the stem. Filament hairs are white, sometimes yellowish; rosette leaves are large; smaller stem leaves are decurrent down the stem. (See also p. 54.)

Prostrate Toadflax *Linaria supina* SCROPHULARIACEAE
A, B or P.6–9. 5–20cm. S.W. Europe, Portugal to Italy.
Occasionally naturalised
This gay little plant, a small procumbent relative of the widespread *L. vulgaris* of roadsides, grows usually on sunny, calcareous stony ground. Its rosettes of creeping stems bear whorls of sessile linear leaves, 1–3cm long, glaucous grey-green. Bilabiate flowers are clear yellow with an orange throat boss and a long down-pointing spur; they grow in short terminal leafless clusters, on stems decumbent to erect.

Bird's-foot-trefoil *Lotus corniculatus* LEGUMINOSAE
P.5–9. 10–40cm. Most of Europe. Grassy places, common.
Despite its variable habit, it is not too difficult to distinguish this plant from its many similar, yellow-flowered, low-growing relatives. Widespread over dry grassland, its rather flat, few-flowered inflorescences range from golden yellow to tawny orange, often streaked or suffused with red. The long, sharply pointed, dark reddish brown seed pods spread from the same point to resemble a bird's foot.

Ploughman's-spikenard *Inula conyza* COMPOSITAE
B or P.7–9. 20–130cm. Most of Europe. Calcareous grassland.
Ploughman's-spikenard's aromatic leaves and roots were once used by poor people instead of expensive ointments from the Far East. The flowering stem arises from a basal rosette of short-stalked leaves; stem leaves are progressively smaller, becoming sessile; all are crinkled above, downy beneath. Numerous, small, composite flower heads crowd into a branched inflorescence, reddish brown and dull yellow.

Meadow Clary *Salvia pratensis* LABIATAE
P.5–8. 30–60cm. C. and S. Europe; introduced N. Grassland.
The brilliant blue, leafless, flowering spikes of this sage are locally dominant. The plant is hairy and aromatic, with crinkled toothed leaves, basal and sparingly on the stem. The whorled flowers are distinctly bilabiate: the upper lip long and curved, the lower horizontal—a good platform for nectar-seeking bees. 2 arched stamens are contained within the hood; a blue style with 2 stigmas projects well beyond.

Spiked Speedwell *Veronica spicata* SCROPHULARIACEAE
P.7–9. 10–60cm. Most of Europe. Calcareous grassland.
This beautiful plant, found locally in sunny places from sea level to 2000m, is distinguished from other *Veronica* species by its solitary, long, tapering spike of densely packed, brilliant blue flowers. Individual flowers are small (*c.* 0.5cm wide), tubular below with 4 spreading lobes from which project 2 long stamens and the style. All leaves are simple, hairy, with crenate margins; lower ones stalked, upper ones smaller, sessile and paired.

Pyrenean Bellflower *Campanula speciosa* CAMPANULACEAE
B.5–7. To 60cm. S.W. Europe, France and Spain. Endemic. Not British.
Usually, although sparingly, found on steep limestone scree, this glorious *Campanula* produces such liberal quantities of large, deep blue bell-flowers that they cover almost the whole plant. They hide the sturdy stems and narrow greyish leaves, leaving only the crowded, long basal leaves visible. A distinguishing feature is the 10-lobed calyx, with 5 long erect sepals and 5 alternating short reflexed ones.

Clustered Bellflower *Campanula glomerata* CAMPANULACEAE
P.6–9. 5–40cm. Most of Europe. Calcareous grassland to 1500m.
Specific and English names give the clue to this plant's characteristic feature—the dense, sessile clusters of rich, dark purple-blue flowers surrounded by leafy bracts, quite unlike the lax spreading inflorescences of most *Campanula* species. These clusters are terminal on the main stem and in upper leaf axils in good specimens; sometimes very short (5cm) 1-flowered plants occur on steep slopes devoid of tall vegetation.

Round-headed Rampion *Phyteuma orbiculare* CAMPANULACEAE
P.7–9. 5–50cm. W., S. and C. Europe. Calcareous grassland.
The spiky inflorescences of Rampions are distinctive in general appearance and in their peculiar flowers, which start as long thin tubes which split into 5 narrow petal lobes (see p. 76). The globular heads of this species sometimes cover sub-alpine meadows and chalk downland with a dark purple-blue haze. The long style and 3 spreading stigmas are blue and project beyond a surrounding tube of anthers, red-orange with pollen.

Chalk Milkwort *Polygala calcarea* POLYGALACEAE
P.5–6. 5–20cm. W. Europe, endemic. Calcareous grassland.
This small member of an attractive genus has a distinctive spreading rosette of short leafy shoots; from the centre grow the flowering stems; below this point stems are leafless. 2 large sepals, blue, pink or white, like the 3 small, enclosed, white-fringed petals, persist, turning green after flowering; variable veining and shape help in identification. The brilliantly blue massed flowers are visible from some distance.

Hairy Violet *Viola hirta* VIOLACEAE
P.3–5. 5–15cm. Most of Europe. Calcareous grassland.
A typical spring-flowering violet of open downland, *V. hirta* differs from *V. odorata* in having no perfume and no creeping stems (stolons) to form new plants. It is distinguished from *V. riviniana* of shady places (p. 76) by its dark purple spur and from both by the overall hairiness of both the leaf stalks and cordate leaves, which are longer than broad. Flowers are usually rich dark violet, occasionally paler.

Field Fleawort *Senecio integrifolius* COMPOSITAE
P.6–7. 7–60cm. Much of Europe; local. Dry grassland.
The leaves of this plant, which is allied to the Ragworts, are a distinguishing feature, being entire, not lobed. Most are basal; stem leaves are few and sessile; when young all are cottony with hairs, which later almost disappear. A single stem carries a few composite inflorescences, spreading stiffly on short stalks radiating from the same point. Each circle of bright yellow ray florets surrounds a disc of darker tubular florets.

Yellow-wort *Blackstonia perfoliata* GENTIANACEAE
A.6–10. 15–45cm. W., S. and C. Europe. Grassland, dunes.
These tall erect plants of dry places may not look like Gentians but they share at least 2 characteristics—paired leaves and the flowers' habit of closing in cloudy weather. The glaucous, grey-green stem leaves are joined across their bases to encircle the stem completely and are larger than those of the basal rosette. Numerous 8-petalled flowers, bright yellow and star-like, spread in loose forked clusters.

Thyme *Thymus vulgaris* LABIATAE
P.4–7. 10–30cm. S.-W. Europe. Endemic. Not British.
Dry sunny hillsides, especially limestone, of southern Spain, France and Italy are the native home of the whitish grey, shrubby plants of this, the true culinary and herbal Thyme, known and used for centuries. The aromatic oils are contained in the numerous, small, linear leaves. This plant is grown in many a garden and is now widely naturalised. Flowers are small, pale purple, clustered.

Autumn Gentian *Gentianella amarella* GENTIANACEAE
B.8–10. 3–25cm. N. and C. Europe. Grassland, dunes.

Chiltern Gentian *Gentianella germanica* GENTIANACEAE
B.8–10. 10–35cm. C. Europe. Local, to 2700m in Alps.
Gentianella displays a silky fringe of hairs at the corolla's throat, distinguishing it from the genus *Gentiana*, which has small lobes between the petals, a feature absent in *Gentianella*. Though variable in size and range, they are both alike in having simple, sessile stem leaves in alternate pairs and both are glabrous. Flowers of *Gentianella* are generally purple, rarely white, with usually 5 (sometimes 4) petals and sepals, often growing in a bushy or tufted manner on short side branches among the upper leaves and leafy bracts.
G. amarella—also called Felwort—is extremely variable in height and branching, with rather small flowers, rich dark purple, sometimes white.
G. germanica is larger, with bigger, paler, bluish purple flowers. In both the green of leaves and stems is often suffused with purple.

Squinancywort *Asperula cynanchica* RUBIACEAE
P.6–7. 8–20cm. Much of Europe, except N. Pastures, dunes.
Squinancywort, named centuries ago for its supposed curative properties for throat ailments, has slender stems, with whorls of narrow, pointed leaves, creeping through short dry grass before ascending to produce spreading clusters of tiny delicate flowers. Pale pinkish white with darker pink veining, they contrast delightfully with the purple Thyme and golden Horseshoe Vetch with which it often grows.

Bloody Crane's-bill *Geranium sanguineum* GERANIACEAE
P.5–8. 15–40cm. Most Europe, except far N. Dry places.
Sometimes locally dominant, this plant indicates the reason for its name with flaunting masses of brilliant purple-red flowers; pale forms occur rarely. Bushy and leafy, the long-stalked, hairy leaves are also distinctive, deeply 5- to 7-lobed, each lobe further divided into 3; all lobes are narrow and pointed. Each flower's 5 spreading petals are finely veined and shallowly notched; 10 stamens have blue anthers; typical 'bird-beak' seed pods follow later.

Military Orchid *Orchis militaris* ORCHIDACEAE
P.5–6. 20–45cm. Much of Europe, except far N. Grassland.
Fairly slender to very robust, the smooth stems and broad, unspotted leaves of this Orchid tone with the softly shaded, greyish lilac flower spikes. The opening buds and flower 'helmets' are pale grey-mauve, the latter striped violet inside; the hanging lips are 3-lobed. 2 upper lobes are narrow, the lowest bluntly lobed again; dark mauve with a spotted centre.

Monkey Orchid *Orchis simia* ORCHIDACEAE
P.4–6. 15–40cm. Mostly S. and W. Europe; local. Grass; scrub.
Similar to the Military Orchid in structure, overall this flower appears more impish and shaggy. The few basal leaves are smaller, glossy and unspotted but both have a few little sheathing leaves higher on the stem. The inflorescence is rounded and denser. The flowers have violet-streaked, silvery pink hoods; the lobes of the purple-spotted lip are dark purple, strap-like and upcurled, resembling tiny monkeys. Rarely white.

Lady Orchid *Orchis purpurea* ORCHIDACEAE
P.4–6. 25–40cm. Much of Europe, especially C. and S. Grass & woods.
In full flower, this is one of Europe's most spectacular Orchids. Proudly erect, it carries a magnificent inflorescence (to *c.* 15cm) of closely packed, lady-like flowers displaying wide crinoline skirts, white with raised maroon spots. The large 5-petalled hood, dark red-purple, is the lady's bonnet, enclosing the similar coloured pollinia; the lip forms the skirt, wide, spreading and often frilly; 2 upper narrow lobes are her arms.

Burnt Orchid *Orchis ustulata* ORCHIDACEAE
P.5–6. 8–25cm. Most of Europe; local. Grassland to 2000m.
A little gem of a plant whose unopened, very dark purple-red buds provide an unusually well-marked, beautiful contrast to the tiny pale flowers below. Stem, leaves, and flower structure resemble those of the 3 species already described but in delicate miniature. The buds and the flower hoods provide the 'burnt' tips; each lip, though tiny, is perfectly formed, with 3 fairly evenly sized lobes, white with red-purple spots.

Common Rock-rose *Helianthemum nummularium* CISTACEAE
P.6–9. 5–30cm. Most of Europe. Calcareous grassland, scrub.

White Rock-rose *Helianthemum apenninum* CISTACEAE
P.5–7. 5–30cm. S. and W. Europe. Limestone rocks, scrub.

Hoary Rock-rose *Helianthemum canum* CISTACEAE
P.5–7. 5–30cm. C. and S. Europe. Rocky limestone pastures.
Small sun-loving relatives of the conspicuous *Cistus* shrubs of the Mediterranean area, *Helianthemum* often grows abundantly, covering boulders and grassy hummocks with rose-like but frail flowers. They are ephemeral, with 5 petals which quickly fall, but fortunately a large production of buds ensures continuity. A long tap root gives firm anchorage and maintains water supply, both necessary in the plants' dry situations. Small linear leaves in pairs are somewhat tufted near the base of the plants and scattered along the flowering stems.
H. nummularium is the commonest and most widespread; its almost sessile, linear leaves are usually green above, white-hairy beneath, with 2 tiny stipules at the base. Large flowers, to 2.5cm across, have bright golden petals, rarely cream, white, or orange-spotted.
H. apenninum is recognised by its large white petals which contrast beautifully with the central cluster of golden stamens common to all species. Leaves and sepals are greyish white with thick hairs, usually on both sides, especially dense beneath; leaf margins are usually incurved.
H. canum is the smallest of these 3 species. Its vegetative parts are hoary grey throughout, with hairs, and the very tiny leaves have no stipules. The bright yellow flowers are only 1–1.5m across and the petals display an attractive tendency to curl backwards.

Woodcock Orchid *Ophrys scolopax* ORCHIDACEAE
P.4–5. 8–40cm. S. Europe. Calcareous. Not British.
O. scolopax includes several subspecies, chiefly confined to the Mediterranean area, showing considerable flower variation. Pictured is the basic type with richly lilac-pink petals: 3 large and spreading, 2 very tiny ones. The rather long, narrow lip, midway between *O. apifera* and *insectifera*, shows a variable assortment of colours and patterns on a velvety red-purple background, with 2 hairy ear-like lobes above and a green appendage below, pointing forward.

Bee Orchid *Ophrys apifera* ORCHIDACEAE
P.5–7. 10–40cm. Much of Europe, not far N. Grassland, dunes.
Possibly the best known of the genus and one of the most beautiful, the flower lip is an excellent imitation of a bumble-bee, rounded, velvety brown, hairy, with variable greenish or yellow loops and spots. Like *O. scolopax*, there are 2 'ear' lobes, but the basal green appendage points backwards. 3 large petals vary from pale to glowing rich lilac-purple, 2 small ones are usually green; rarely all are white.

Fly Orchid *Ophrys insectifera* ORCHIDACEAE
P.5–7. 15–50cm. Much of Europe. Widespread.
Small, dark, distantly spaced flowers render the Fly Orchid less conspicuous than most *Ophrys* species. The only bright part is a broad blue band centred across the red-brown, 3-lobed lip, representing the fly's body. The hooded dark column resembles the head. The lip is notched, with no appendage and, as with all *Ophrys* species, no spur. 3 spreading outer petals are green; 2, very thin, inner ones are brown.

Red Helleborine *Cephalanthera rubra* ORCHIDACEAE
P.5–7. To 60cm. Much of Europe, local. Light woodland.
Quite unmistakable, with its large flowers, richly shaded from rose-red to lilac, *C. rubra* brings the occasional exotic touch to shady places. The slightly downy stem has about 6, smooth, pointed leaves below a loose spike of 3–10 flowers, each perched on its twisted ovary. 6 almost equal segments spread fairly wide. The lip is beautifully ridged, with yellow touches, narrowing below to a sharply pointed tip.

Columbine *Aquilegia vulgaris* RANUNCULACEAE
P.5–6. 40–100cm. W., C. and S. Europe. Woods and wet places.
This tall graceful plant has slightly glaucous, ferny leaves and nodding flowers ('Granny's Bonnets') of deep purple-blue. Large, long-stalked, basal leaves are 3-lobed, again divided partway; upper stem leaves are sessile and tripartite. 5 petaloid sepals, usually blue, rarely white or pale pink, spread around an inner circlet of 5, shorter, similar-coloured petals, each ending in a nectar-containing spur, curved at the tip.

No English name *Aphyllanthes monspeliensis* LILIACEAE
P.4–7. 20–50cm. S.W. Europe. Dry stony places. Not British.
These slender-stemmed plants which produce a glorious display of massed blue flowers are deceptively strong, tufted and anchored in stony ground by a hard root stock. From this arise numerous, wiry, flowering stems, sheathed at the base by a few insignificant leaves. The flowers emerge from a terminal cluster of papery bracts and spread, star-like, 6 rounded petals of purple-suffused blue; they close in rain.

Purple Gromwell *Buglossoides purpurocaerulea* BORAGINACEAE
P.4–6. 30–60cm. S. and C. Europe, Britain, S.C. Russia. Scrub, wood margins.
Like many Boraginaceae, this plant exhibits a marked contrast between rough, hairy, vegetative growth and brilliant flowers, which open from red-purple buds through purple to white-centred vivid blue; to 2cm across, they spread in loose, terminal, forked clusters. Long, creeping runners give rise to numerous erect leafy flowering stems, ensuring a glorious, though local, display.

Pyramidal Orchid *Anacamptis pyramidalis* ORCHIDACEAE
P.5–8. 10–50cm. Most Europe except far N. Grassland.
The pyramidal shape of this orchid's neat inflorescence is a guide to identification. Flowers and leaves are unspotted, the latter rather short and broad, sheathing and pointed. The spiral arrangement of orchid flowers, giving each adequate space and light, is perfectly displayed. Flowers are rich reddish purple, with a hood, 2 short side-petals, an evenly 3-lobed lip and a long, narrow, downward-pointing spur.

Fragrant Orchid *Gymnadenia conopsea* ORCHIDACEAE
P.5–7. 15–60cm. Almost all Europe. Calcareous grassland.
Widespread, sometimes abundant, the long, slender, flowering spikes of this plant are strongly scented. Like *Anacamptis*, flowers and leaves are unspotted, but leaves are long and narrow. Flowers have a very small hood, 2 longer horizontal side petals, a short, shallowly 3-lobed lip and an even longer, down-pointing, distinctly curved spur. Flowers are rosy pink to lilac-purple, occasionally white.

Musk Orchid *Herminium monorchis* ORCHIDACEAE
P.5–7. 5–20cm. Much of Europe; not Atlantic. Grassland.
Ground level is the best viewpoint for these scattered small slender Orchids as their overall light green colour merges with that of flowering grasses. Usually 2 fairly broad leaves sheathe the stem's base, with perhaps 1–2 tiny ones above. The somewhat unilateral flowering spike contains about 10–30 small, drooping, yellow-green flowers, sweet-scented and bell-shaped; the lip has a long central lobe; there is no spur.

Frog Orchid *Coeloglossum viride* ORCHIDACEAE
P.6–8. 6–35cm. Europe. Widespread. Grassland, to 2700m.
The Frog Orchid tolerates a wide habitat range, from calcareous dunes and downland to mountains, and so shows much variation. From entirely green to reddish brown—this especially in mountain plants—there are all shade combinations between. All leaves are sessile and unspotted; lower ones broad, upper ones smaller and linear. Flowers are small, with a short spur and unmarked lip whose central lobe is tiny.

Mountain Everlasting *Antennaria dioica* COMPOSITAE
P.5–6. 6–20cm. Much of Europe. Dry grassland to 3000m.
Also called Catsfoot and Pussypaws because of its rounded, furry flower heads, this charming plant is dioecious, the female displaying the longest plumes. Stems and leaves' undersides are thickly hairy; most leaves form a basal rosette, are spathulate, green above; stem leaves are small and linear. Each flower head is surrounded by small papery persistent bracts, from white to deep pinkish red; those on the male flowers resemble small rounded petals.

Spring Sandwort *Minuartia verna* CARYOPHYLLACEAE
P.5–9. 5–15cm. Much of Europe. Dry stony places; calcareous.
Sandworts are a confusing group, the name being used loosely for plants of several genera. This pretty, spring-flowering type produces tufted cushions, thick with tiny, moss-like leaves and comparatively large, starry, white flowers. These grow singly on short, forked branches (as in many Caryophyllaceae), have 5 rounded petals and usually 10 stamens with pink anthers. Interestingly, it grows freely near disused lead mines.

Biting Stonecrop *Sedum acre* CRASSULACEAE
P.6–7. 2–10cm. Most of Europe. Grassland, walls, dunes.
The succulent Stonecrops are plants of dry sunny places where their numerous spreading branches will rapidly cover much ground. In *S. acre*, short, sessile, cylindrical, glossy leaves overlap one another tightly to make a thick mat-like covering, which in summer is hidden by masses of gloriously golden, 5-petalled, starry flowers. The leaves have a strong peppery taste, hence the alternative name of Wall-pepper.

Stinking Hellebore *Helleborus foetidus* RANUNCULACEAE
P.2–5. 20–80cm. S.W. Europe to Britain. Calcareous scrub and wood-margins.
Tall, rather untidy, strong-smelling, highly poisonous, yet at flowering time, the contrast between overwintering leaves and light spring green of numerous pendant cup-like flowers is very pleasing. Lower leaves are palmately divided into 9, narrow, serrated lobes; upper ones reduced to simple blades, sometimes lobed at the top. 5 petaloid sepals, tipped with dark red, enclose a bunch of yellow stamens and 3–5 green pistils.

Man Orchid *Aceras anthropophorum* ORCHIDACEAE
P.6–7. 15–40cm. Chiefly W. and C. Europe. Grassland.
Although of similar overall greenish colouring to Musk and Frog Orchids (p. 112) this plant is usually much taller. Most leaves (about 6) are basal, broad, unspotted, glossy and sheathing. The flower spike is long, narrow, with rather small, drooping, green flowers, usually red-tinged. The 5-petalled hood represents the man's head, bending above the long narrow lip, whose 4 narrow divisions are like arms and legs.

Lizard Orchid *Himantoglossum hircinum* ORCHIDACEAE
P.5–7. To 90cm. Most of Europe. Grassland, open woods.
The long waving 'tongues' of the Lizard Orchid are peculiarly distinctive, like the tall pale plant itself, whose large floppy leaves droop early. The flowers, from 15–80 in a long fairly lax spike, each have a 5-petalled, grey-green hood, streaked with red. The lip lies neatly coiled in bud but unwinds like a living spring into a narrow twisted strap, about 5cm long, with 2 short, curled, lateral lobes.

Pasqueflower *Pulsatilla vulgaris* RANUNCULACEAE
P.4–5. 10–30cm. Chiefly N.W. and C. Europe. Dry grassland.
The Pasqueflower or Easter-flower is very beautiful. Each single erect flower with 6, glorious, royal purple sepals and vividly contrasting centre of golden stamens nestles in a setting of finely bipinnate, fern-like leaves, springing directly from the rootstock. Except for the flower's inner surface, the whole plant is covered with soft silvery hairs. The delicately plumed seed head droops from the lengthened stalk.

Greater Knapweed *Centaurea scabiosa* COMPOSITAE
P.7–9. 30–90cm. Most of Europe. Calcareous grassland.
The Knapweeds resemble Thistles, but most, like this one, lack spines. Their variability means identification is not always easy. Points to watch include the degree of leaf division and fine details of the fringed involucral bracts. This species is widespread, often abundant, usually branched, with large purple inflorescences wider than the involucre and long, lobed, outer florets. Leaves are deeply pinnatifid and toothed.

Sainfoin *Onobrychis viciifolia* LEGUMINOSAE
P.6–8. 30–60cm. C. Europe; naturalised elsewhere. Grassland.
A good fodder plant, Sainfoin is widely cultivated and now naturalised in many places. Its bushy growth and masses of rich pink flowers are frequently dominant. Leaves are pinnately divided into several, narrow, sharply pointed leaflets; densely flowered long-stalked racemes grow erect from the leaf axils. The typical leguminous flowers are streaked with red; sepal lobes are hairy, very long and narrowly pointed.

Purple Milk-vetch *Astragalus danicus* LEGUMINOSAE
P.5–7. To 35cm. Britain, Denmark, S. Sweden to S.W. Alps.
This charming plant occurs locally on northern sea cliffs and dunes and hill and mountain pastures farther south on calcareous ground. Low-growing, it is clothed with numerous, delicate, pinnate leaves, silvery grey with hairs, each with about 7–10 pairs of small simple lobes. The rounded to oval inflorescences, of about 8, tightly clustered, softly blue-violet flowers, grow singly on slender erect stalks.

White Flax *Linum suffruticosum* LINACEAE
P.5–7. To 50cm. S.W. Europe; Spain to Italy. Dry hills, rocks. Not British.
The slender branching stems and delicate flowers of this lovely Flax contrast surprisingly with its rather shrubby base. Plants in sheltered places are compactly rounded, the stems clothed with tiny stiff leaves, linear and pointed. Large flowers open from long furled buds, renewed each day as they quickly fall; they are 5-petalled, white with softly violet or pink centres, in branched spreading clusters.

Autumn Lady's-tresses *Spiranthes spiralis* ORCHIDACEAE
P.8–10. 7–20cm. S., W. and C. Europe. Grassland.
Sometimes in quantity, sometimes few, flowering late in the year, this pale grey-green plant appears almost ghost-like in short autumnal grassland. As tiny buds open from the base, the definite spiral of greenish white, spurless flowers curls neatly around the stem. Its peculiarity lies in the production of a lateral, basal leaf rosette during or after flowering in readiness for next year's growth.

Wayfaring-tree *Viburnum lantana* CAPRIFOLIACEAE
P.4–6. 2–6m. C. and S. Europe. Scrub, open woods, hedgerows.
Attractive and unusual features of this shrub are the buds, protected by a number of folded, felty, grey-green leaves. Stems and mature leaves are also felted hairy, the leaves especially thick beneath and deeply wrinkled on both sides, with saw-toothed margins. Creamy flowers are massed into slightly convex, wide inflorescences, followed by fairly large, clustered berries, green, then red, finally glossy black.

Blue Hound's-tongue *Cynoglossum creticum* BORAGINACEAE
B.3–6. 30–80cm. S.E. Europe. Mediterranean.
This plant displays characteristics typical of Boraginaceae e.g. biennial growth beginning with a ground rosette of long-stalked leaves, overall hairiness, numerous flowers in curving inflorescences. The large basal leaves presumably resemble hounds' protruding tongues; stem leaves become progressively smaller and sessile; grey-green. Pale blue flowers, streaked with violet, have 5 petals outspread above a short tube and are followed by fruits consisting of 4 spiky nutlets.

Dropwort *Filipendula vulgaris* ROSACEAE
P.6–8. 15–50cm. Most of Europe; not Arctic. Grassland.
One of the loveliest sights of chalk downland and lime-based meadows is the massed delicate flower heads of Dropwort above surrounding vegetation. Although not scented, like the related Meadowsweet, *F. ulmaria*, it is much daintier with numerous ferny leaves, mostly basal, whose alternate leaflets are prettily and unevenly dentate. Tiny rosepink-tipped buds unfold into creamy 6-petalled flowers with many yellow stamens, clustered loosely in irregular inflorescences.

Traveller's-joy *Clematis vitalba* RANUNCULACEAE
P.6–8. To 30m. S., W. and C. Europe. Woods and hedgerows.
This tough climber develops stems thick as a man's wrist, using its sensitive leaf stalks to pull itself successfully over shrubs and trees. By contrast, the leaves have simple triangular lobes; flowers are dainty with 4 felty-backed green sepals and numerous slender stamens. Later the plumed seed heads appear silvery in slanting autumn sunlight; Old-man's-beard in winter when the silver becomes fluffy grey.

Spindle *Euonymus europaeus* CELASTRACEAE
P.5–6. Frt. 9–12. To 6m. Most of Europe. Bushy places.
Throughout most of the year, this shrub or small tree is rarely noticed with its smooth grey bark, simple pointed leaves and small, green, 4-petalled flowers drooping in loose clusters. During autumn, when its leaves become bronze-red and the deep pink fruits are further brightened as they split to reveal 4 brilliant orange seeds, it reigns supreme.

Agrimony *Agrimonia eupatoria* ROSACEAE
P.6–9. To 60cm. Most of Europe. Dry grassland.
Agrimony's tall slender spikes of small, yellow, rose-like flowers are readily seen amongst shorter brighter plants. Usually stems are single, occasionally with a few erect branches, bearing several attractive ferny leaves, pinnately divided, with very small leaflets between the large normal ones. The inflorescence spike, to 20cm long, has many flowers, less crowded below, followed by characteristic, hairy, ridged seed heads which become brown and dry, with hooked bristles around the top.

Dark-red Helleborine *Epipactis atrorubens* ORCHIDACEAE
P.6–8. 15–40cm. Much Europe; local. Calcareous rocky slopes.
Though their common names may cause confusion, this plant is quite distinct from the Red Helleborine (p. 110). Usually later-flowering, its shorter, broader, leaves are keeled, in 2 rows and often purplish-tinged. The flowers, 8–18, in a tighter spike, are short-stalked, pendulous and warm brick red in colour. They are fairly wide open, with a short broad lip, showing brighter red bosses and a small reflexed tip.

Melancholy Thistle *Cirsium helenioides* COMPOSITAE
P.7–8. 45–120cm. Most of Europe. Calcareous grassland.

Woolly Thistle *Cirsium eriophorum* COMPOSITAE
B.7–9. 60–150cm. W. and C. Europe. Calcareous grassland.

Dwarf Thistle *Cirsium acaule* COMPOSITAE
P.7–9. Usually stemless. Most of Europe. Calcareous grassland.
Thistles are widespread and well known, with their characteristic prickly leaves and mostly purple, composite flower heads. These 3 species differ in habit but are basically similar. All have spirally arranged leaves, usually pinnately divided or lobed with prickly margins. The conspicuous inflorescences are composed of numerous, densely packed, small, tubular florets; seeds are plumed feathery 'thistledown'.
C. helenioides has an unbranched cottony grey stem and undivided leaves, saw-edged but not spiny, felted with hairs underneath. Large solitary inflorescences are usually held erect, the purple florets outspread well beyond the purple-tipped involucral bracts.
C. eriophorum is exceptionally cobwebby, branched above, with soft stem hairs. The leaves are divided into about 4 rows of forward-pointing bristly lobes, green above, woolly beneath, each ending in a very sharp spine. The florets form a comparatively small, flattish, purple pad above a beautifully patterned globe, with many sharp, purple, evenly spaced spines connected by densely cobwebbed hairs.
C. acaule grows almost hidden amongst grass, its spiny, dark green leaves, flat to the ground in a spreading rosette, often several plants together. Centred in each rosette is a rich purple inflorescence, usually stemless.

Musk Thistle *Carduus nutans* COMPOSITAE
B.5–8. 20–100cm. Mostly W. and C. Europe. Fields, waysides.
This handsome thistle is distinguished by its drooping inflorescences, solitary on separate stalks. They are large, to 7cm across, with rich red-purple, tubular florets in a slightly rounded, dense head, backed by sharply spiny bracts, the outer ones reflexed and all frequently purple-tipped. Leaves, some way below the flowers, are deeply lobed and sinuate; the very spiny margins are decurrent partway down the stem.

No English name *Carduncellus mitissimus* COMPOSITAE
P.5–7. To 10cm. S.W. and C. France, N.E. Spain. Not British.
These lovely non-prickly plants of stony ground are frequently stemless with a large lilac-purple inflorescence nestling in the centre of a rosette of finely pinnate leaves. Long tubular florets have 5, narrow, spreading petal lobes and a long, protruding, purple style, surrounded by 5 creamy white anthers. The innermost involucral bracts are reddish and fringed; the outer ones have slightly leafy, green tips.

Moss Campion *Silene acaulis* CARYOPHYLLACEAE
P.6–8. Arctic-alpine. Widespread; abundant to 3700m.
The Traveller's-joy of the mountains—from tiny-flowered, sparse plants to massed, glorious, rose-pink cushions and cliff-hanging cascades, Moss Campion in full flower never fails to delight the alpine walker. Wild winds, eroded soil, shattered rocks, snow and hail—it survives them all with a long tap root, close-packed moss-like leaves and vivid (occasionally white) flowers.

Sweet-William Catchfly *Silene armeria* CARYOPHYLLACEAE
A or B.7–9. 10–60cm. C. and S. Europe. Naturalised elsewhere. To 1200m.
As beautiful as Moss Campion, this plant, confined to lower ground, shows more readily visible *Silene* characteristics. Simple, paired, glabrous leaves clothe erect, pale green stems, branched above to display dense, flat-topped clusters of deep pink flowers; 5 notched petals spread above a long, slightly inflated, 5-pointed calyx, streaked with red. 10 stamens and 3 longer styles crowd the corolla's narrow throat.

Alpine Sow-thistle *Cicerbita alpina* COMPOSITAE
P.7–9. 50–180cm. C. Europe to 2200m; N. Europe to 1300m.
In contrast to most alpine plants, this handsome species is large in all ways: height, numerous leaves to 25cm long, densely flowered racemes to 30cm tall. Lower leaves are deeply lobed; the terminal lobe is biggest, triangular and pointed; all are irregularly toothed. Rare enough in Britain to be legally protected, elsewhere it clothes bushy mountain slopes with massed flowers, opening from the top downwards, purplish blue in sunlight, darker blue in shade.

Pyrenean Thistle *Carduus carlinoides* COMPOSITAE
P. 6–8. To 50cm. Pyrenees. Stony ground to 2500m. Not British.
This prickly thistle is silvery grey before flowering, with a mass of closely packed buds centred in a spreading rosette of narrow leaves, deeply divided into numerous lobes ending in long, exceedingly sharp spines. As the buds expand into rosy purple flower heads, to 2cm across, the winged stems lengthen, giving a branched bushy effect, with spreading flower clusters above spine-tipped, woolly-haired bracts.

Androsace *Androsace villosa* PRIMULACEAE
P.6–7. 3–10cm. S., C. Europe. Rocks; 1200–3000m. Not British.

Alpine Androsace *Androsace alpina* PRIMULACEAE
P.7–8. C. Alps. Endemic. Rocks above 2000m. Not British.
The many delightful Androsaces are true mountain plants with similar basic characteristics: pink or white 5-petalled flowers, with tiny throat scales; small simple leaves in rosettes or dense tufts.
Silky-haired *A. villosa* has tufted leaf rosettes and short, leafless stems, each with a small crowded umbel of delightfully variable flowers, white to pink with yellow or deep pinkish red centres.
A. alpina, one of the most glorious of the genus, clings to narrow ledges and tiny cracks in lime-poor rocks with snowfields and glaciers never far away. Its compact cushions of small hairy leaves, from 2–20cm across, are often completely covered at flowering time, presenting a wonderful rockbound picture of pale rose-pink, each single, almost stalkless flower enhanced by a golden centre.

Rock Soapwort *Saponaria ocymoides* CARYOPHYLLACEAE
P.5–7. To 20cm. S.W. and S.C. Europe. Endemic. To 2000m. Not British.
Although *Saponaria* forms large ground-hugging masses of pink 5-petalled flowers it is not related to *Androsace*. Its habitat range, on stony ground, is lower and its stems are loosely trailing. Finely hairy, like the stems, the leaves, 1–4cm long, are in pairs, subtending the branching flowering stalks. A long-veined reddish calyx tube splits into 5 lobes.

Black Vanilla-orchid *Nigritella nigra* ORCHIDACEAE
P.6–8. 5–25cm. Mountains to 2800m. Not British.

Rosy Vanilla-orchid *Nigritella nigra* ssp. *rubra* ORCHIDACEAE
P.5–7. 5–25cm. Alps; Carpathians. 1600–2500m. Not British.
The most widespread and perhaps best loved of all mountain orchids are
charming plants with unusual, dark wine-red flowers, appearing almost
black at a distance before the buds are fully open. Stems and leaves are
yellow-green, the former slightly furrowed, the latter narrow, grass-like
and glossy, spirally arranged and sheathing at the base. The tightly
packed inflorescences may contain 50, small, star-like flowers, whose
petals are more regular in size and arrangement than in most orchids. The
lip, also unusually, points upwards and the spur is short and blunt. Both
emit a delightful fragrance of vanilla. *N. n.* ssp. *rubra* has flowers of a more
glowing red than its relative, in longer inflorescences; petals are broader
and the lip, still pointing upward, is the broadest of all.

House-leek *Sempervivum tectorum* CRASSULACEAE
P.6–8. 10–60cm. C., S. Europe. To 2800m. 0m.

Large-flowered House-leek *S. grandiflorum* CRASSULACEAE
P.7–9. 10–30cm. Swiss and Italian Alps. Endemic. 1300–2500m.
House-leeks love the sun. Rosettes of succulent leaves sit tight on rocks,
walls and scree, usually in family clumps of varying ages. The rosettes
persist for several years, rooting and spreading by stolons; eventually each
produces one erect, leafy flowering stem before dying. Large red, pink or
yellow flowers grow in terminal branched clusters; 8–16 star-like petals
spread open to sun and warmth.
S. tectorum is the largest and most widespread species, once frequently
planted on house roofs—to keep the tiles in place or to give protection
against lightning, thunderbolts and witches!
S. grandiflorum, local and uncommon, displays an attractive colour
arrangement. Its hairy leaves are deep- or yellow-green with red tips and
its long, narrow, pointed petals are pale yellow with purple-red centres,
matched by the stamen filaments.

Alpine Lady's-mantle *Alchemilla alpina* ROSACEAE
P.6–8. 10–20cm. Arctic-alpine. Rocky places to 3000m.
The beautiful silvery appearance of Alpine Lady's-mantle amply com-
pensates for its inconspicuous petal-less flowers. Often thickly spread
over stony ground, leaves and flowers grow separately from a creeping,
woody root stock; each leaf is divided, usually to the base, into 5 or 7 lobes,
mid-green above and silky hairy beneath. The branched flower stalks are
longer than those of the leaves and bear distantly spaced, dense clusters of
tiny greenish yellow flowers.

Net-leaved Willow *Salix reticulata* SALICACEAE
P.6–8. To 8cm. Arctic-alpine. 1300-2500m. Damp rocks.
The fascinating Mountain Willows, the tiniest trees in the world, have all
the physical features of a complete tree in miniature. Roots, twiggy stems
with annual rings, leaves and catkins are all compressed into less than 8cm
of aerial growth. This species is distinguished by its beautifully net-
veined leaves, often in extensive carpets, which are woolly when young,
later becoming dark green above.

Box-leaved Milkwort *Polygala chamaebuxus* POLYGALACEAE
P.5–9. 5–12cm. W. and C. Europe. To 2500m. Not British.
This attractive undershrub is widespread on stony slopes and in light
mountain woodland, forming gaily coloured carpets. Creeping woody
stems produce numerous, glossy, evergreen leaves, to 1.5cm long, with
sharply pointed tips. Amongst the upper ones grow 'butterfly' flowers
whose sepals ('wings') are usually yellowish white and petals ('keel') clear
bright yellow; forms with pink or maroon wings are sometimes found. In
both types, the keel finally turns brownish orange.

Alpenrose *Rhododendron ferrugineum* ERICACEAE
P.6–8. 30–90cm. Not N. Stony slopes. Not British.
There are 2 species of *Rhododendron* in Europe's mountains, separated by differences in their leathery evergreen leaves. This species is named from the resinous rust-coloured glands covering the undersides; its counterpart on calcareous ground, *R. hirsutum*, exhibits instead a marginal fringe of hairs. Both are devices to conserve water. The lovely clustered flowers are tubular, 5-lobed and deep pink.

Alpine Sainfoin *Hedysarum hedysaroides* LEGUMINOSAE
P.7–8. 10–25cm. S.-C. Europe, Arctic USSR, Urals. Not British.
Locally common on stony mountain pastures, Sainfoin is not unlike a small lupin, with a long tapering raceme of large flowers. Trailing stolons give rise to erect flowering stems, from which the loosely crowded, leguminous, red-purple flowers droop unilaterally. They overtop numerous attractive pinnate leaves with 5–9 pairs of narrow oval leaflets, darker above. The winged, jointed seed pods have 2–5 separate segments.

Flesh-pink Lousewort *Pedicularis rostrato-spicata*
SCROPHULARIACEAE
P.7–8. 15–45cm. E., C. and W. Alps. 1500–2700m. Not British.

Leafy Lousewort *Pedicularis foliosa* SCROPHULARIACEAE
P.7–8. 20–60cm. C. Europe. To 2500m. Not British.
Several Louseworts range from lowlands to mountains; partially parasitic on roots of grasses, they all have colourful flowering spikes. Frequent hybridisation complicates identification but the group is readily recognisable. The numerous, pinnate, fern-like leaves have serrate lobes; flowers are bilabiate, the upper lip arched and often strongly beaked (a guide to identification), the lower lip 3-lobed and spreading. The whole inflorescence is a mingling of flowers and leafy bracts.
P. rostrato-spicata has long, rose-pink inflorescences overtopping narrow leaves. The upper lip is strongly beaked, darker than the wide shallowly divided lower one.
P. foliosa is exceptionally leafy, including the inflorescence. Flowers are pale yellow; the upper lip, though curved, is not beaked and the lower one quite deeply divided.

Giant Knapweed *Leuzea rhapontica* COMPOSITAE
P.7–8. 40–100cm. C. Europe. 1400–2600m. Not British.
Despite its thistle-like inflorescence, this non-spiny plant is not a true Thistle. An erect stout stem rises from a base of long, serrate leaves, greyish hairy below, like the few small stem leaves. The terminal flower head is packed with tubular, purple florets with protruding styles and stigmas. Below, the involucre has a regular spiral design of rounded-triangular, parchment-like bracts with notched martins.

Alpine Willowherb *Epilobium fleischeri* ONAGRACEAE
P.7–9. From 15cm. E., C., W. Alps; local, endemic. Not British.
This bushy plant has strong creeping stems with numerous ascending branches, clothed with narrow, dark green, sessile leaves, slightly serrate. Large showy flowers are borne in terminal clusters on stalks shorter than the elongated ovaries. 4 narrow spreading sepals, dark greenish purple, alternate with 4 broad rose-purple petals; style and 10 stamens purple.

Fairy Foxglove *Erinus alpinus* SCROPHULARIACEAE
P.5–10. 5–15cm. S., S.-C. Europe. To 2400m. Introduced to Britain.
This beautiful little plant of rocky places, especially mountain cliffs and ledges, spreads rapidly if naturally seeded, or planted, on stone walls and bridges. Its growth is low and tufted, with several erect flowering stems arising from a loose leafy rosette. All leaves are spathulate, almost sessile and crenate in the upper half. The flowers, in terminal clusters, display variable shades of pinkish purple—rarely white—with 5, spreading, notched petals.

Alpine Aster *Aster alpinus* COMPOSITAE
P.7–8. 8–30cm. C. Europe. 1500–3200m. Not British.
This easily recognised plant exhibits great variation in height, flower colour and width of ray florets. It grows among short meadow-grass in posy-like clusters; each stem bears 1 inflorescence with a golden centre of perfect tubular florets surrounded by a circlet of ray florets, pink, lilac, purple or—rarely—white; occasional rayless forms occur. Leaves are simple, linear, sessile or nearly so.

Pyrenean Fritillary *Fritillaria pyrenaica* LILIACEAE
P.6–7. 15–30cm. S.C. France, N.W. Spain. 500–2000m. Not British.
Related to the Snakeshead Fritillary of water meadows, this species is confined to a few mountain areas on high steep grassland. Each single-stemmed plant produces a few short, narrow, glaucous leaves and 1–2 large, pendant, bell-shaped flowers, with 6 reflexed petals, very variable in colour. Outwardly they are dark, chequered, ranging through chocolate-brown to maroon-violet; inside, greenish yellow and maroon.

Matted Globularia *Globularia cordifolia* GLOBULARIACEAE
P.5–7. 4–6cm. Widepsread to 2600m. Not British.

Leafless-stemmed Globularia *G. nudicaulis* GLOBULARIACEAE
P.6–8. 8–30cm. Pyrenees, Alps. To 2700m. Not British.
The obvious characteristic of this genus is the inflorescence, solitary, rounded and composed of a densely packed head of small, tubular, misty mauve-blue florets. These are 2-lipped; the lower larger one displays 3, long, narrow spreading lobes, giving the inflorescence an attractive deeply fringed appearance. *Jasione montana* (p. 52) has similar flower heads and grows up to 1700m, but has campanulate 5-lobed corollas and is not woody.
G. cordifolia, also evergreen, forms extensive and beautiful mats of soft blue flowers mingled with shining, dark green, spathulate leaves, all in tufted low growth from creeping woody stems. Both these species are found in stony grassy places in calcareous soils.
G. nudicaulis holds its large flower heads aloft on long, smooth leafless stems, well above the basal rosette of glossy evergreen leaves.

Pyramidal Bugle *Ajuga pyramidalis* LABIATAE
P.5–7. 5–20cm. Much of Europe, chiefly mts. 1300–2800m.
When young, this plant is distinctly pyramidal in shape, the pyramid elongating somewhat as the flowers develop. It is very hairy, and, except for a few large basal greenish leaves and the pale blue, bilabiate flowers, the whole plant is dull reddish purple in colour. Crowded, horizontal, sessile stem leaves gradually merge into leafy bracts which subtend and almost hide very small flowers.

Dark Rampion *Phyteuma ovatum* CAMPANULACEAE
P. 6–8. 50–90cm. S. Europe. To 2400m. Not British.
This Rampion is unmistakable with long, dark, blackish violet flower spikes in sharp contrast to the surrounding vegetation. The basal leaves are large, cordate, long stalked; the stem leaves become gradually smaller, narrower and sessile; all are irregularly toothed and pointed. Inflorescences are narrow and tightly packed with shaggy flowers, displaying the typical *Phyteuma* structure: petals united when young, separating first in the middle, finally at the top.

Wild Carnation *Dianthus superbus speciosus* CARYOPHYLLACEAE
P.6–8. 30–60cm. Europe, not extreme W. and S. To 2400m. Not British.
This superb *Dianthus* grows in rough meadows and woody hills. The mountain form, shown here, has especially large flowers. Stems and paired linear leaves are glaucous; each branch ends in a long, pointed, inky blue bud which opens to a beautiful 5-petalled fragrant flower, delicate pale pink, rarely white. Each petal is deeply and finely fringed; the centre is flecked with green and soft with reddish hairs.

Mountains

Orange Lily *Lilium bulbiferum* LILIACEAE
P.6–7. 30–60cm. C. Europe. To 2400m. Not British.

Martagon Lily *Lilium martagon* LILIACEAE
P.6–8. 30–90cm. Much of Europe to 2800m. Naturalised British Isles.
'If you have two loaves, sell one and buy a lily' says an Eastern proverb.
But which lily—amongst the many strikingly beautiful ones typified by
these two mountain species?
L. bulbiferum is perhaps the most brilliant of all the alpine plants, its vivid
flame-coloured flowers proudly erect on bouldery sun-baked slopes. The
stems are clothed with numerous linear leaves in whose axils small bulbils
sometimes grow, able to reproduce new plants without fertilisation.
Petals, stamens and pistil are all glowing orange, yellow, and red.
L. martagon has flower spikes which extend above whorls of short, fairly
broad leaves, and contain up to about 36 drooping flowers which, in bud,
are beautifully cobwebbed with white hairs. Open flowers are darkly
spotted on soft deep pink, rarely white, with petals reflexed away from the
prominent orange-red style and stamens.

Wild Tulip *Tulipa sylvestris* ssp. *australis* LILIACEAE
P.4–7. 12–30cm. Mainly S., E. Meadows to 2000m. Not British.
The shining flowers of Wild Tulip, open wide in sunshine, provide an
enchanting picture. The stems are slender and flexuous but strong, green
in the lower half, brownish purple above; leaves are 2 in number, short,
linear and glaucous. Small but typical tulip flowers have 6 pointed petals,
bright golden yellow within; the 3 outer ones are reddish outside, the 3
inner ones yellow outside with a median red stripe.

Glacier Wormwood *Artemisia glacialis* COMPOSITAE
P.7–8. 5–15cm. S.W. Alps. Endemic, rare. 1900–3100m.
This species, the most beautiful aromatic *Artemisia*, is found sparingly
high up on screes, moraines and stony slopes. From leafy cushions grow
erect flowering stems with terminal, short-stalked inflorescences of
crowded, tiny, tubular florets surrounded by brown-edged bracts. The
silvery green of stems and small finely cut leaves, due to a thick covering of
silky hairs, contrasts with the vivid gold, rounded flower heads.

Alpine Avens *Geum montanum* ROSACEAE
P.5–7. 10–20cm. Most European mts, not N. 1600–2800m.

Creeping Avens *Geum reptans* ROSACEAE
P.6–8. 10–15cm. Alps to Carpathians. 2000–3800m. Not British.
These similar plants possess reddish almost leafless stems, each with 1
large terminal yellow flower; from 6–8 separate petals are backed by a
double calyx, green in *G. montanum*, red in *G. reptans*.
G. montanum is widespread over large areas of stony mountain grassland,
where its deep yellow flowers are followed by the most delicately beautiful
of all alpine plumed seed heads, with persistent feathery styles shining
silvery red in the sunlight. The leaves, mostly basal, are pinnately
divided, the terminal leaflet much the largest, and all further lobed.
G. reptans, less common, brings glorious splashes of brilliant colour to the
stoniest of moraines and scree, where it maintains its existence by means
of long creeping stolons (not found in *G. montanum*). The terminal leaflets
are only slightly larger than the lower ones and the silvery red seed plumes
display a distinctive spiral twist.

Swiss Treacle Mustard *Erysimum helveticum* CRUCIFERAE
P.6–7. 2–12cm. Alps, Pyrenees, Balkans. Not British.
This plant of stony terrain varies considerably in height according to the
austerity of its situation. In the dwarf alpine form, vivid compact flower
clusters may completely hide the small, linear, finely hairy leaves. Leaves
and flowering stems grow from a tough, woody root stock, which provides
firm anchorage in often unstable ground. Large 4-petalled golden flowers
resemble Wallflowers and show the typical cruciferous structure.

Snowy Medlar *Amelanchier ovalis* ROSACEAE
P.4–5. 1–3m. S. and C. Europe. To 2400m. Not British.
At flowering time, this deciduous shrub presents a most attractive picture amongst the green of light sub-alpine woods and rocky slopes. When fresh, the oval, finely toothed leaves are downy-white beneath. These, with the numerous creamy white flowers, give the wood a dappled, snowy appearance. Later the leaves become green and hairless; the long, narrow, waving petals fade; bluish black pulpy sweet berries follow.

Rock Snapdragon *Antirrhinum sempervirens* SCROPHULARIACEAE
P.6–7. 15–30cm. C. Pyrenees; E.C. Spain. Endemic. To 2000m.
The shrubby stems of Rock Snapdragon, at first procumbent, become erect against cliff faces to enable the terminal clusters of paired flowers to turn outwards to the light, yet the root-run to remain cool and moist. On the stems grow several pairs of short oval to linear hairy leaves. Creamy flowers are bilabiate: the broad lower lip 3-lobed, the upper with a distinctive plum-coloured blotch.

No English name *Saxifraga paniculata* SAXIFRAGACEAE
P.5–9. 10–30cm. C. and S. Europe. To 2700m. Not British.

Purple Saxifrage *Saxifraga oppositifolia* SAXIFRAGACEAE
P.4–8. To 30cm. Arctic-alpine. Sea level to 3800m. Widespread.

Mossy Saxifrage *Saxifraga bryoides* SAXIFRAGACEAE
P.6–8. 3–8cm. S. and C. Europe. 2000–3700m. Not British.
Saxifrages can thrive to an extraordinary degree in the harshest climatic conditions and the most difficult stony terrain. They comprise one of the most typical and specialised genera of high mountain plants and display great diversity of form and colouring; often a profusion of starry, 5-petalled flowers completely hides the tiny leaves.
S. paniculata usually grows in rock crevices and on cliff ledges where its tight, leafy rosettes form large colonies, extending by creeping runners. Leaves are simple, leathery, bluish green, with toothed margins encrusted with lime. Loose clusters of creamy white flowers grow from the upper half of glandular hairy stems.
S. oppositifolia is one of the most glorious of the high alpines, flowering in brilliant profusion immediately following the melting snow. Large flowers, from pink to deepest purple, grow from trailing or hanging wiry stems, thick with dark green, lime-encrusted leaves, fringed with hairs.
S. bryoides is a typical 'mossy' Saxifrage, growing from rosettes of fine moss-like leaves, green with sharp hairs. Crowded slender stems are leafy, bearing 1–2 large, yellow cream flowers with broad rounded petals. This is one of the highest-growing alpines, shunning lime.

Alpine Poppy *Papaver sendtneri* PAPAVERACEAE
P.6–8. 5–15cm. C. and E. Alps. 1200–3000m. Not British.
Despite its dainty and delicate appearance, the small white Alpine Poppy is strong enough to live amongst the stoniest debris in the windiest places at considerable heights. Its long-stalked basal leaves are deeply lobed and slightly bluish with silvery hairs on both sides. Flowers are solitary on slender stalks; from 2 protective, hairy sepals emerge 4 thin petals, at first crumpled, later spreading cup-shaped around the pistil and stamens.

Mountain Avens *Dryas octopetala* ROSACEAE
P.5–8. 3–8cm. Arctic-alpine. Sea level to 2700m; widespread.
Sunny places based on limestone are the home of these beautiful spreading plants. Their woody stems creep beneath a carpet of evergreen leaves, indented, shining, dark green and deeply veined above, felted with fine white hairs beneath. The flowers, 3cm across, are borne singly on slender, hairy stalks and possess 8 sepals, usually 8 white petals—occasionally to 24—and numerous stamens and pistils. They are followed by equally beautiful feathery seed heads.

Feather-grass *Stipa pennata* GRAMINEAE
P.5–7. 30–60cm. C., S. Europe. Stony grassland. Not British.
This beautiful and extraordinary grass is distinguished by its ingenious mechanism of seed dispersal. A 25cm-long, feathery plume parachutes the pointed seed through the air and when it falls, it is gradually pushed into the ground by the hygroscopic action of a tough wiry spiral just behind it. Because its pointed tip is slightly hooked, the seed stays firm while this is taking place.

Yellow Bellflower *Campanula thyrsoides* CAMPANULACEAE
B.7–9. 20–30cm. Jura, Alps, Balkans. 1500–2700m. Not British.
The crowded blunt-topped spikes of this unusual Bellflower grow amongst grass on bouldery hillsides. The lower part of the erect stem is thickly clothed with bristly-haired simple linear leaves; above, the pale yellow campanulate flowers are dense enough to present a solid broad spike. The lower bells are interspersed with long leafy bracts projecting almost horizontally, like the yellow styles.

Mont Cenis Bellflower *Campanula cenisia* CAMPANULACEAE
P.7–9. 1–5cm. Alps; moraines, scree. 2000–3500m. Not British.
Of the many small rock-hugging, high-growing Bellflowers, this one is local and rare. Its long roots and creeping stems produce neat tufted rosettes of hairy leaves and short, leafy flower stalks. Attractive deeply furrowed buds unfold into large slaty blue flowers. The corolla has 5 star-like spreading lobes, reflexed to reveal 5 stamens and a prominent style with 3 creamy stigmas.

Bearded Bellflower *Campanula barbata* CAMPANULACEAE
P.6–8. 10–35cm. Alps, S. Norway. 1000–2500m. Not British.
With porcelain-blue flowers drooping from an erect hairy stem, often in a unilateral raceme, this is one of the gems of mountain grassland. Most leaves form a basal rosette; long, simple, hairy especially beneath. The short reflexed corolla lobes are delicately whiskered with a criss-cross pattern of fine white hairs. The hairy calyx has 5, long, pointed sepals alternating with 5 short, reflexed ones, with distinct blue-black blotches around the base.

Fairy's-thimble *Campanula cochlearifolia* CAMPANULACEAE
P.6–8. 5–20cm. S. Europe. To 3000m. Not British.
This dainty plant resembles a diminutive version of Harebell. Its basal leaves are fairly broad and toothed; those on the slender stems are very narrow; all are glabrous. Frequently, hundreds of soft mid-blue bells line mountain road verges and decorate any stony place from walls to river gravel and forbidding cliffs with glorious hanging posies of blue.

Mont Cenis Restharrow *Ononis cristata* LEGUMINOSAE
P.6–8. 5–35cm. S.W. Alps, C. Appenines, E. Spain. To 1800m.
One of the smallest Restharrows, this non-spiny, mat-forming plant is uncommon and local. Short, erect flowering stems, slightly woody at the base, have numerous, bright green, trifoliate leaves with large leaf-like sheathing stipules. The somewhat ovate leaflets are distinctly toothed around the wide end; in the upper leaf axils grow long-stalked solitary flowers, clear rose pink or with white wings and keel.

Trailing Azalea *Loiseleuria procumbens* ERICACEAE
P.6–8. To 10cm. Arctic-alpine. 1150–3000m. Exposed moors.
This tough ground-hugging shrub spreads woody stems (reported as living for at least 55 years) widely over the stony terrains of high exposed acid moors and plateaux. Tiny, evergreen, leathery leaves, with margins strongly recurved beneath to control water evaporation, form extensive brown-green carpets. During the short summer, these carpets are threaded with thousands of small, starry pink flowers.

Aconite-leaved Buttercup *Ranunculus aconitifolius*
RANUNCULACEAE
P.6–8. 30–100cm. C. and S. Europe. To 2600m. Not British.
Pyrenean Buttercup *Ranunculus pyrenaeus* RANUNCULACEAE
P.5–7. 10–20cm. Alps, Pyrenees, Spain, Corsica. To 2600m.
Not British.
Alpine Buttercup *Ranunculus alpestris* RANUNCULACEAE
P.6–7. 3–12cm. S. Europe. 1700–2800m. Not British.
Glacier Crowfoot *Ranunculus glacialis* RANUNCULACEAE
P.7–8. 5–15cm. Arctic-alpine. 2300–4275m. Not British.
The showy cup-shaped flowers of Buttercups are widespread in Europe,
usually yellow on the plains, white in water and on the higher mountains,
brilliantly variable around the Mediterranean. Typically, the flower has
distinct petals and sepals (sometimes falling early) and numerous stamens
and pistils.
R. aconitifolius abundantly dapples moist meadows and shady places with
a multitude of large flowers on widely branching stems. Buds are pinkish
red, with sepals falling as the white petals unfold. Lower leaves are large
and long-stalked, smaller and sessile on the upper stem and all deeply
divided into 3–5 toothed lobes.
R. pyrenaeus is much smaller with unbranched stems and solitary flowers.
It also dapples wet grassland, but in higher pastures, closely following the
winter snow. The slightly bluish leaves are linear, somewhat shorter than
the flowering stems. Sepals are green. Sometimes double-petalled forms
occur but the petals can be disappointingly ephemeral.
R. alpestris is similar in size to *R. pyrenaeus* and overflows from stony
pastures to damp rocky crevices, mostly calcareous. It is readily distinguished by its leaves: basal, rather small, long-stalked, rounded and lobed,
each lobe divided more shallowly. Sepals are green and petals slightly
notched and frilly.
R. glacialis is the highest recorded flowering plant in Europe, at 4725m on
the Swiss Finsteraahorn. It is a glorious plant, never far from glaciers and
perpetual snow, with glossy stems and leaves—hairy at the greatest
heights. Large flowers (3.5cm) open white and change through pink to soft
red after pollination. Sepals are hairy, brownish red and persistent.

No English name *Callianthemum coriandrifolium*
RANUNCULACEAE
P.7–8. 10–20cm. S. Europe; rare. 1800–3000m. Not British.
The attractive leaves of this plant provide a useful identification feature.
Basal and long-stalked, except for 2 sessile stem leaves, all are glaucous,
pinnate and intricately lobed; when young they are tightly furled and
imbricate. The conspicuous solitary flowers are simple and very white;
5–12 spreading petals are somewhat square-ended and golden centred; 5
narrow sepals are sometimes pinkish.

Spiniest Thistle *Cirsium spinosissimum* COMPOSITAE
P.7–9. 20–50cm. Alps, Apennines. To 3100m. Not British.
An aptly named plant which is nevertheless quite attractive at flowering
time, growing in scattered clumps on poor stony grassland. Large leaves,
deeply pinnate with prickly margins and long, spine-tipped lobes, clasp
the erect ridged stems. Pale straw-coloured flowers cluster tightly in
composite heads, about 20 in a terminal inflorescence, the central head
flowering first. The whole is surrounded by even paler, extremely spiny,
long bracts.

Spring Crocus *Crocus vernus* IRIDACEAE
P.3–6. 2–10cm. C., S. Europe. 800–2500m. Introduced to British Isles.
One of the thrills of spring-time is to see myriads of purple and white
Crocuses flowering around, even through, the melting snow of mountain
pastures. Cup-like flowers, closed in cloudy weather, spread out 6 petals
in response to the sun's warmth, revealing a golden centre of 3 stamens
and 3 feathery stigmas, attractions for early flying bees. At the same time,
the leaves appear, stiff and grass-like with a white central line.

Ramonda *Ramonda myconi* GESNERIACEAE
P.6–8. 5–15cm. Pyrenees; N.E. Spain. To 1800m. Not British.
Ramondas are quite distinctive. Their large rosettes of thick leaves spread from damp cliff crevices and around bouldery hollows; the leaves are dark green, strongly crinkled above, rusty hairy beneath, with bluntly toothed, hairy margins. From the rosette's centre grow several reddish stems carrying one or a few clustered flowers, intensely rich violet in colour. 5 broad petals spread flat around a centre of protruding style and contrasting golden stamens.

Alpine Flax *Linum alpinum* LINACEAE
P.5–8. 10–30cm. Pyrenees to N. Urals. To 2000m. Not British.

Sticky Flax *Linum viscosum* LINACEAE
P.6–8. 30–60cm. S. and S.C. Europe. To 2200m. Not British.
The best known Flax is the blue-flowered *L. usitatissimum*, cultivated for linen and linseed oil. There are many wild species, however, characterised by small, linear, sessile stem leaves, usually alternate, and the ephemeral nature of their petals, which fall daily; fresh flowers appear the next morning.
L. alpinum is not unlike its cultivated relative but much smaller—except the flowers—and is a true mountain plant, widespread though local on stony limestone pastures. Large sky-blue flowers are borne erect in loose clusters on long slender smooth stalks which tend to droop at the fruiting stage.
L. viscosum is a tufted plant with usually pink, delicately veined flowers growing on very short stalks in rather long narrow clusters. The upper leaves, bracts and sepals are all glandular hairy and sticky.

Pyrenean Columbine *Aquilegia pyrenaica* RANUNCULACEAE
P.6–8. 10–30cm. Pyrenees, N. Spain. Endemic. 1500–2500m.
The mountain columbines look generally similar, but usually grow in distinct localities, which helps identification. The Pyrenean plant is slender and delicate with long-stalked radical leaves, tripartite and lobed. Flowers are almost translucent and clear soft blue; sepals are large and outspread and the petals comprising the inner circlet are rounded. Spurs are straight or slightly curved.

King-of-the-Alps *Eritrichium nanum* BORAGINACEAE
P.7–8. To 8cm. Alps, rare, local. 2500–3600m. Not British.
This cushion-plant usually grows on sparkling granite, rarely far from the perpetual snowline in the High Alps, where it is strongly protected. Growing on exposed rock-faces and in fissures, the Forget-me-not-like flowers often hide the mat of tiny, silvery, long-haired leaves beneath. Cushions of up to 250 very short-stalked flowers may be found—of an exquisite azure blue (rarely white) with golden centres.

Pyrenean Hyacinth *Brimeura amethystina* LILIACEAE
P.5–7. 10–30cm. Pyrenees, N.W. Yugoslavia. To 1800m.
Formerly known as *Hyacinthus*, this slender-stalked bulbous plant graces open, stony, steep mountain grassland. The long leaves are basal, narrow, grass-like and smooth; the single, erect flowering stem ends in a loose rather 1-sided raceme of 3–12 bell-shaped flowers, short-stalked, drooping and delicately pale blue with 6 short spreading lobes.

Rock Speedwell *Veronica fruticans* SCROPHULARIACEAE
P.6–8. 5–15cm. Arctic-alpine; Scotland. 600–3000m.
The Rock Speedwell flourishes on exposed granitic rocks where its brilliant blue flowers are displayed to perfection. From a woody base grow slender stems with several pairs of almost sessile, oval to linear leaves and a loose terminal cluster of flowers. These have 4, slightly unequal, large petals and only 2 stamens; the white centre is surrounded by a thin red ring, a distinguishing mark of this species.

Small-white Orchid *Pseudorchis albida* ORCHIDACEAE
P.6–8. 12–30cm. Much of Europe, chiefly mts. To 2500m.
This fragrant Orchid grows in pastures and rough meadows, sometimes amongst shrubs and light woodland. Stem and leaves are glossy; most leaves are basal, unspotted and fairly broad. The spike is densely crowded with creamy white flowers, each like a helmet above a short 3-lobed lip, the central lobe being the largest. The short thick spur curves downward; ovaries and subtending bracts are equal in length.

Veratrum *Veratrum album* LILIACEAE
P.7–9. 60–90cm. Much of Europe, rare N. To 2700m. Not British.
When flowering, this tall robust plant is unmistakable; at other times it may be confused with *Gentiana lutea*. Both have single leafy stems with broad sessile leaves, strongly ridged; but those of *Veratrum* are alternate and downy beneath, while the Gentian's leaves are paired and somewhat glaucous. Veratrum's flowers appear in dense, leafless panicles; they are sessile with 6, spreading, star-like, green petals.

Yellow Gentian *Gentiana lutea* GENTIANACEAE
P.6–8. To 120cm. C., S. Europe; To 2500m. Not British.
Quite unlike the typical gentian, *G. lutea*— the source of a medicinal tonic, and also 'Enzian' liqueur, which was extracted from the roots—has short-stalked bright yellow flowers growing in leafy whorls at intervals up the unbranched stem. The 5–9 narrow petals, united at the base, are shaggily outspread. Both Gentian and Veratrum are abundant in alpine and sub-alpine grassland.

Tansy-leaved Rocket *Hugueninia tanacetifolia* CRUCIFERAE
P.6–8. 30–65cm. S.W. Alps, Pyrenees, N. Spain. 1700–2500m. Not British.
This attractive small-flowered meadow crucifer has deeply divided, ferny leaves, reminiscent of those of Tansy but not fragrant. Tough, erect, finely hairy stems are leafy all the way, each long leaf pinnate with irregularly dentate lobes. Small, bright yellow, 4-petalled flowers are borne in conspicuous massed clusters on upper side branches, producing a slightly convex spreading inflorescence.

Trumpet Gentian *Gentiana clusii* GENTIANACEAE
P.5–8. To 10cm. C. and S. Europe. 1200–2700m. Not British.

Spring Gentian *Gentiana verna* GENTIANACEAE
P.4–8. 3–9cm. C. and S. Europe; British Isles. To 3000m.
These Gentians provide a glorious display of blue-dappled mountain grassland—one of the greatest floral delights of all Europe.
G. clusii has large trumpet flowers which nestle in the grass pointing to the sun; but close, like most Gentians, when it disappears. Usually a rich dark blue, they are sometimes lightly spotted inside; sepals are erect, straight sided; rosette leaves are rather leathery with pointed tips.
G. verna is the earliest-flowering Gentian and leads us to the High Alps, where shorter, similar, equally brilliant species take over. Small leaves spread in a flat rosette, short stems have 1–2 leaf pairs; solitary flowers spread 5 petals wide and flat above a long narrow tube, their glorious blue enhanced by a clear white centre. Most Gentians produce pale or white flowers occasionally.

No English name *Astragalus centralpinus* LEGUMINOSAE
P.7–8. 50–100cm. S.W. Alps; S. Bulgaria. 500–2000m. Not British.
What fascinating plants these are, perched on steep rocky slopes like beautiful furry Lupins. Bushy, with several stems, numerous, long, pinnate leaves and crowded inflorescences, they are densely silvery hairy throughout, except the upper leaf surfaces. Inflorescences open from the base upwards; a single plant displays all stages intermingled: silver-green buds, fluffy sepals turning soft brown-red around pale yellow corollas, and furry grey seed heads.

Jove's Flower *Lychnis flos-jovis* CARYOPHYLLACEAE
P.6–8. 40–90cm. Alps, endemic, local. 1000–2000m. Not British.
The soft grey woolly coat of this plant helps to conserve water in its dry
rocky habitat and is a foil for the brilliant flowers, crowded into terminal,
almost flat-topped, inflorescences of rich rose-carmine. Erect unbranched stems and paired simple leaves, mostly sessile, are thick with hairs;
the 5, large, deeply notched petals are pink-fringed at the throat.
Sometimes cultivated and found naturalised.

Alpine Soldanella *Soldanella alpina* PRIMULACEAE
P.4–7. 5–15cm. C.S. Europe. 1200–3000m. Not British.
In early spring, Soldanellas, the most dainty of alpine flowers, bloom in
countless numbers through and around the retreating snow, transforming
the soggy grassland into a misty-purple carpet. Dark reddish stems arise
from rosettes of stalked, rounded, shining leaves (the 'little coins' of its
name), and each stem carries from 1–3 drooping lilac-purple (rarely
white) flowers, deeply and beautifully fringed.

Red Alpine Primrose *Primula hirsuta* PRIMULACEAE
P.4–6. 5–10cm. Alps; C. Pyrenees. 1500–3000m. Not British.
There are many mountain species of pink and purple *Primula* growing by
bouldery streams and waterfalls, on stony grassland and ledges, and
poking from narrow cracks and crevices. *P. hirsuta* is sometimes abundant
and is variable, according to situation. Its large lovely flowers are deep
rosy pink with white centres; leaves are thick, leathery, glandular hairy
with toothed margins.

Meadow Saffron *Colchicum autumnale* LILIACEAE
P.8–10. 5–15cm. Most of Europe, except extreme N. To 2000m.
The Meadow Saffron has developed a peculiar life cycle. Its lovely silvery
purple flowers colour autumn meadows and produce seeds which do not
ripen until the following spring, when fat green capsules (4cm) appear
just above ground level within a circle of large glossy leaves. Seeds are
dispersed and leaves withered before autumn returns. Sometimes named
Autumn Crocus, it differs from that genus in the leaves and the possession
of 6 stamens and 3 separate styles.

Bear's-ear *Primula auricula* PRIMULACEAE
P.5–7. 5–20cm. Alps, Carpathians, Apennines. 800–2800m.
A glorious yellow *Primula* of the high mountains, found usually on steep
wild cliffs and quite different from the pale Oxlip of the lower pastures. Its
large leaves are variably mealy, sometimes thickly so; margins vary from
entire to crenate usually with a limy encrustation. Each single sturdy stem
is crowned with a cluster of clear yellow fragrant flowers worthy of legal
protection.

Sticky Primrose *Primula latifolia* PRIMULACEAE
P.6–7. 3–18cm. Alps; Pyrenees. Endemic. 1800–3000m.
Like *P. hirsuta*, this plant has suffered from frequent name changes. It
grows in similar situations but much less commonly. Very large leaves,
soft but stickily glandular, wavy-edged and lightly crenate, surround the
single erect stem with its usually unilateral Cowslip-like umbel of up to 20
flowers. These are rich violet-purple; mealy, but not white at the throat.
All these Primulas tend to hybridise.

Mountain Pansy *Viola lutea* VIOLACEAE
P.5–8. 3–16cm. W. and C. Europe; British Isles. To 2000m.
This Pansy adorns large areas of mountain grassland and nestles vividly
on dark cliff ledges; its creeping rhizomes ensure its colourful continuity.
The leaves vary from rounded (lower) to almost linear (upper), crenate
with lobed leafy stipules. Slender stems produce exceptionally large
flowers in all shades of purple and bright yellow, separately or mingled,
with dark honey guides at the centre.

Large Yellow Foxglove *Digitalis grandiflora* SCROPHULARIACEAE
B or P.6–8. E., C. Europe; Pyrenees, Alps. Not British.
Although not common, excellent stands of this handsome Foxglove occur locally on wayside verges and steep banks. Tall and stately, like its woodland relatives (p. 68), erect leafy stems grow from rosettes of large radical leaves. Each stem terminates in a long spike of pendant bell-shaped flowers, slightly bilabiate, twice the size of those of *D. lutea* and delicately patterned inside with a red-brown network of veins.

Christmas-rose *Helleborus niger* RANUNCULACEAE
P.12–5. 8–15cm. Alps, Carpathians, N. Apennines. To 1850m.
It is wonderful to discover Christmas-roses amongst melting snow and wintry trees. Creamy or pinkish white, exquisite drooping buds above the colder white of the snow; large wide open flowers, golden-centred with stamens, and the first glossy leaf. Later the flowers turn green as large seed pods develop; more short-stalked leaves appear, with 7–9 fingers spreading over the wet ground. Protected.

Anemone *Anemone narcissiflora* RANUNCULACEAE
P.6–7. 20–40cm. S.C. Europe; Urals. 1500–2600m. Not British.
Though local, this plant sometimes dominates large areas of damp calcareous grassland with its large beautiful flowers, borne in terminal umbels and subtended by lobed leafy bracts. The larger, long-stalked, radical leaves are similarly palmately lobed and softly hairy. Flower buds are dark red, gradually becoming paler until the fully opened flowers are white inside, flushed pink on the outside. Seed heads are hard, green, not plumed.

Snowdon Lily *Lloydia serotina* LILIACEAE
P.6–7. 5–15cm. Alps to Urals; N. USSR; Wales. 900–3000m.
Though apparently fragile, the Snowdon Lily grows in high wild places, scattered singly over rough grass and cliffs and on the very edge of rocky mountain torrents. It is one of the few bulbous high alpines, with a slender stem and long grass-like leaves. The dainty white flower (usually 1, sometimes 2) is 6-petalled, cup-shaped to spreading, and delicately etched with lines of yellow and brownish red.

Alpine Toadflax *Linaria alpina* SCROPHULARIACEAE
A, B or P.6–8. 10–20cm. C. and S. Europe. Not British.
The glorious trailing mats of Alpine Toadflax are found, at the greatest heights, on screes, rocks, moraines and glacier river-gravel, locally in quantity and visible from several metres. The small bluish leaves are closely whorled on the lower stems, a muted foil for the brilliant flowers, whose violet-purple petals and spurs are usually offset by the bright orange (sometimes pale purple) boss.

No English name *Vitaliana primuliflora* PRIMULACEAE
P.5–7. 3–6cm. Alps, Pyrenees, Apennines. Not British.
Closely related to *Androsace*, this low-growing plant forms vivid gold patches on high mountain grassland, screes and rocks. Creeping woody stems are closely packed with rosettes of numerous, very tiny, pointed leaves, greyish green and covered with short star-like hairs. Comparatively large (1.5cm) primula-like flowers cluster in loose groups above the leaves; 5 clear yellow petals spread above a long tube. Local, usually avoiding lime.

Hacquetia *Hacquetia epipactis* UMBELLIFERAE
P.4–6. 10–25cm. E. Alps to N. Carpathians. Not British.
From the creeping rhizomes of this inconspicuous local plant of mountain woodland grow long-stalked leaves and erect leafless stems, each with a crowded umbel of tiny yellow flowers, surrounded by large leafy bracts. Single large leaves are palmately divided into 3–5 wedge-shaped leaflets, each further lobed and toothed. The whole plant is thus an unusual attractive harmony of shining yellow-green.

Alpine Anemone *Pulsatilla alpina* RANUNCULACEAE
P.6–7. 10–35cm. S. and C. Europe. 1000–2800m. Not British.

Spring Anemone *Pulsatilla vernalis* RANUNCULACEAE
P.4–6. 2–4cm. Sub-arctic-alpine. 1300–2750m. Not British.
P. alpina bespangles stony lime-based meadows and hillsides with large milky white flowers held above fern-like leaves. These are mostly basal, long-stalked, deeply lobed and toothed, lightly hairy; smaller sessile leaves encircle the stem midway. Petals, about 8, are spreading, white within, softly hairy and suffused grey-blue outside, and wonderfully translucent in sunlight.
The gay yellow counterpart of the Alpine Anemone, *P. a. apiifolia*, is usually found on granite. Both vary in size according to situation and altitude; both exhibit large, closely packed, plumed seed heads. Each seed has a long reddish plume, silvered with a covering of short hairs, especially dense at the base.
P. vernalis is flowering in abundance on wet pastures where patches of deep snow still lie, before its alpine relatives appear. The silky-haired stems are short; the leaves, just appearing, are lobed but not fern-like; the ice-blue-white unfolding buds and wide opalescent flowers are countless. The petals are white inside and delicately pinkish lilac outside; there is a collar of furry bronze bracts.

St Bernard's Lily *Anthericum liliago* LILIACEAE
P.5–6. 20–60cm. Much of Europe. Hills; sub-alpine to 2000m.
This page is graced by 2 related and ethereally lovely plants, the St Bernard's and St Bruno's Lilies, which show many similarities. Both favour steep dry stony slopes, but the latter is more restricted in distribution and altitude. Both produce a few grass-like leaves, about as long as the flowering stem, which, in *A. liliago*, carries a long terminal raceme of up to 15 pure white flowers whose 6 petals, about 3cm long and narrow all their length, spread wide like a star.

St Bruno's Lily *Paradisea liliastrum* LILIACEAE
P.6–8. 30–50cm. Pyrenees, Alps, Jura, Apennines. 1700–2500m. Not British.
Reaching greater heights than St Bernard's Lily, and frequently on the steepest stony hillsides, this Lily differs in its slightly sturdier appearance and slightly broader leaves. The white fragrant flowers are fewer (2–6) and larger (to 5cm long), held almost horizontally in a unilateral raceme. The petals rarely spread star-like; narrow at the base, they widen gradually into a graceful 6-pointed funnel.

Edelweiss *Leontopodium alpinum* COMPOSITAE
P.7–8. 3–10cm. C. and S.E. Europe. 2000–3000m. Not British.
The fascination of Edelweiss lies in its exceptionally dense covering of soft white hairs and in the legendary romance surrounding its stark rocky mountain home. Its flannel-like coat is practical, conserving water, but certainly adds to its attraction. The flower heads contain 5–10 small inflorescences, each with several tiny florets and all surrounded by large pointed furry bracts which attract pollinating insects.

Photography

Plant-hunting with a camera is an exciting and sometimes risky operation as the objects of our desire frequently abide in almost inaccessible places. Recording a tiny Bog Orchid only 10cm tall involves lying flat in soggy wet moss and focusing from a distance of 15–30cm. As the stinking, icy cold water percolates through to very personal locations, the photographer must nevertheless concentrate on the subject as it is the photograph that matters! After climbing a steep cliff face with our apparatus, having first identified a plant with binoculars, it becomes a test of agility, with an element of risk, to secure a rewarding photograph of the specimen.

Photographing wild flowers *in situ* is not something that can be done hurriedly; time and patience are needed, to choose the best plant or group and to select the most suitable background, sometimes sky or water, dark trees or light-coloured rock. Ideally, the flower should be shown clearly in its natural setting and 'gardening' should be kept to a minimum and entail no damage. It is advisable to take several pictures, from general habitat to close-ups; note that buds and seed heads can add valuable information to the picture, as can rain drops, ice crystals and nectar-hunting insects. A confusing background can be eliminated by the use of a matt black cloth held sufficiently far behind the plant to prevent its pattern being reproduced.

The photographs were taken with an Exakta, the original single-lens, waist-level reflex camera using extension tubes for macro-shots with a 50mm Zeiss Pancolor lens. Production of this model ceased nearly 50 years ago but, rarely, it is still available second-hand. It has been succeeded by the wide range of Praktica cameras with similar characteristics and modern gadgets.

I do not use a tripod (Marjorie refuses to carry one!) but rocks and tree stumps often serve the same purpose. Small low-growing plants are usually best 'attacked' lying flat on the ground, when I myself am the tripod.

As our photography is undertaken from early morning to late evening and in all weather conditions, I consider electronic flash to be an essential accessory. This factor overcomes poor light, eliminates wind movement and offers considerably better depth of focus. Meticulous accuracy in focusing is necessary, especially with macro-shots, when depth of field is minimal. Watch the background; chalk, light rock and sand can cause over-exposure as the intensity of the flash is bounced back. The flash unit is best used independently and sideways from the camera, as direct flash can cause flare. Using natural light, *contre-jour* pictures of certain flowers render dramatic results, but experience is needed to avoid flare and a working partner can help by shading the lens. Allow also for the fact that red, blue, purple and green flowers absorb light whereas white and yellow ones reflect it. Natural sunlight is ideal, but it limits this type of photography to the middle of the day whereas electronic flash can be used in all conditions, including deep shade, high winds and even during rain and blizzards. Film speed and the power of the flash-gun dictate the F stop but, for macro-shots, the key is experience as camera lenses and flash guns vary. I normally use Kodachrome 25 and my flash gun has a factor of 40 with this film. Experience prescribes a stop between F8 and F22, depending on distance from subject, flower colour and background.

Seeking and identifying wild flowers in their natural habitat, coupled with photography, tests one's stamina and patience to the limit. In predicting the whereabouts of rarities, our crystal ball is made up of a lot of hard thinking, research and hard work but it has to be polished with a bit of good luck from time to time.

Conservation

'The wildlife of today is not ours to dispose of as we please. We have it in Trust and must account for it to those who come after.'

King George VI

In these times, much is said and written about the conservation of wildlife, including plants. Fortunately much is also being done, although not yet enough. As with all worthwhile objectives, the cost is high—in money, time, energy and even the sacrifice of certain amenities.

Plants tend to be overshadowed by the appeal of the larger animals and exotic birds, but it should never be forgotten that, without plants, neither they nor we could continue our earthly existence. The whole animal kingdom is completely dependent upon them, for only plants can manufacture the food products essential to us all. This they do by the marvellous process of photosynthesis, the interaction of sunlight with their own green chlorophyll, and all mankind's agriculture and food production are founded upon this basic phenomenon.

Plants possess other worthwhile qualities, however. Their beauty, variety and astonishing tenacity in the most difficult situations provide us with constant joy and wonder. For all these reasons we should be prepared to pay a high price for wildlife conservation.

Most European countries now accord some legal protection for wild plants, including Great Britain where the Wildlife and Countryside Act 1981 lists 62 species (only 21 in the previous 1975 act) as being fully protected against interference of any kind, while none may be uprooted without the landowner's permission. In Europe, many plants, especially alpines, are legally protected; each country has its own laws.

Also on the credit side, and happily so, is the provision of National Parks and Nature Reserves throughout Europe and Great Britain where wildlife communities can live unmolested, yet where people may wander, watch and learn. Botanic gardens, established in many places, from cities to the mountains, give specific care for plants and provide opportunities for scientific research. Many of these incorporate information and display centres to help visitors to learn and benefit from the life of these wonderful wild places.

In addition, many enlightened landowners and farmers now willingly set aside part of their land specifically as nature reserves or, where possible, manage the whole estate so that wildlife is given some measure of protection and freedom.

National and local conservation organisations, of which there are many, welcome membership and assistance from interested people. By the amassed help of individuals good worthwhile work can be done and is being done, with splendid—even worldwide—results!

Bibliography

BELLAMY, D. (1976) *Bellamy's Europe* BBC, London

CHRISTIANSEN, M.S. (1974) *The Pocket Encyclopaedia of Wild Flowers In Colour* Blandford Press, Poole

CLAPHAM, A.R., TUTIN, T.G. & WARBURG, E.F. (1962) *Flora of the British Isles* Cambridge University Press

CULPEPER, N. (1968) *Complete Herbal* Foulsham, Slough, Berkshire

FITTER, R., FITTER, A. & BLAMEY, M. (1974) *The Wild Flowers of Britain and Northern Europe* Collins, London

GJAEREVOLL, O. & JØRGENSEN, R. (1963) *Mountain Flowers of Scandinavia* Trondhjems Turistforening, Trondheim

GREY-WILSON, C. (1979) *The Alpine Flowers of Britain and Europe* Collins, London

HALLIDAY, G. & MALLOCK, A. (Eds) (1981) *Wild Flowers. Their Habitats in Britain and Northern Europe* Eurobook, London

HEGI, G. (1930) *Alpine Flowers* Blackie, London

HEPBURN, I. (1952) *Flowers of the Coast* Collins, London

HEYWOOD, V.H. *et al.* (1978) *Flowering Plants of the World* Oxford University Press

HOLDEN, A.E. (1952) *Plant Life in the Scottish Highlands* Oliver & Boyd, Edinburgh

HUTCHINSON, J. (1972) *British Wild Flowers* Volumes 1 and 2. David & Charles, Newton Abbot

HUXLEY, A. (1967) *Mountain Flowers in Colour* Blandford Press, Poole

HUXLEY, A. & TAYLOR, W. (1977) *Flowers of Greece and the Aegean* Chatto & Windus, London

HYDE, H.A. & WADE, A.E. (1957) *Welsh Flowering Plants* National Museum of Wales, Cardiff

JAEGER, P. (1961) *The Wonderful Life of Flowers* Harrap, London

KLEIJN, H. & VERMEULEN, P. (1964) *The Beauty of the Wild Plant* Harrap, London

LANDOLT, E. (1975) *Geschützte Pflanzen in der Schweiz* [Protected Plants in Switzerland] 2nd Edition. Schweizerischer Bund for Naturschutz, Basle

LOUSLEY, J.E. (1971) *Wild Flowers of the Chalk and Limestone* 2nd edition. Collins, London

MARTIN, W. KEBLE (1976) *The Concise British Flora in Colour* Ebury Press and Michael Joseph, London

PARISH, D. & M. (1979) *Wild Flowers; a Photographic Guide* Blandford Press, Poole

PERRING, F.J. & WALTERS, S.M. (Eds) (1976) *Atlas of the British Flora* 2nd edition. E.P. Publishing (Botanical Society of the British Isles) Wakefield

POLUNIN, O. (1969) *Flowers of Europe* Oxford University Press

POLUNIN, O. & HUXLEY, A. (1965) *Flowers of the Mediterranean* Chatto & Windus, London

POLUNIN, O. & SMYTHIES, B.E. (1973) *Flowers of South-west Europe* Oxford University Press

PRAEGER, R. LLOYD (1974) *The Botanist in Ireland* E.P. Publishing, Wakefield

RARĂU-BICHICEANU, R. & BICHICEANU, M. (1964) *Flowers of Rumania* Meridiane Publishing House, Bucharest

RAVEN, J. & WALTERS, M. (1956) *Mountain Flowers* Collins, London

SCHROETER, C. *Alpen-Flora* 27th edition. Raustein Verlag, Zurich

STOCKEN, C.M. (1969) *Andalusian Flowers and Countryside* Stocken, Devon

SUMMERHAYES, V.S. (1968) *Wild Orchids of Britain* 2nd edition. Collins, London

TAYLOR, A.W. (1971) *Wild Flowers of the Pyrenees* Chatto & Windus, London

THOMPSON, H. STUART (1911) *Alpine Plants of Europe* Routledge, London

THOMPSON, H. STUART (1912) *Subalpine Plants* Routledge, London

THOMPSON, H. STUART (1914) *Flowering Plants of the Riviera* Longmans, Green, London

TOSCO, U. (1974) *The World of Mountain Flowers* Orbis, London

TUTIN, T.G. *et al.* (Eds.) (1976) *Flora Europaea* Cambridge University Press

VARESCHI, V. & KRAUSE, E. (1947) *Mountains in Flower* Lindsay Drummond, London

WILLIAMS, J.G., WILLIAMS, A.E. & ARLOTT, N. (1978) *A Field Guide to the Orchids of Britain and Europe* Collins, London

Glossary

Achene A small dry single-seeded fruit, often several in a head.
Acuminate Narrowing gradually to a point, e.g. of leaf of sepal.
Annual A plant which grows, sets seed and withers within 12 months.
Annual ring Circular mark in cross-section of trunk indicates 1 year's growth.
Anther Upper part of stamen which contains pollen.
Arctic-alpine A plant found in the Arctic and mountains.
Asexual Reproduction of a plant without pollination.
Auricle Small ear-like projection at base of leaf.
Awn Stiff bristle-like projection in grass flowers.
Axil Angle between a leaf or bract and the stem.
Basic or base-rich Soil largely calcareous.
Biennial Plant with 2-year life cycle, flowering in the second year.
Bifid Lobed deeply into 2 parts.
Bilabiate Irregular corolla, with 2 distinct lips.
Brackish Salty, of wet places.
Bract Small leaf-like structure, from the axil of which a flower often grows.
Bracteole Small secondary bract.
Calcareous Rock containing much calcium carbonate, i.e. chalk, limestone.
Calcicole A plant usually growing on chalk or lime-based soil.
Calcifuge A plant not normally growing on lime-based ground.
Calyx The sepals as a whole, whether free or united.
Capsule A dry fruit, which usually splits to release the seeds.
Carpel A single section of the ovary or fruit.
Cartilaginous Tough and hard, like cartilage.
Catkin A cluster of tiny flowers, often tassel-like, frequently on trees or shrubs.
Chlorophyll The green colouring matter of plants.
Column Structure in the centre of an Orchid flower, formed by the fusion of stamens, style and stigma.
Contiguous Touching at the edges, e.g. petals.
Cordate Heart-shaped.
Corolla The petals as a whole, whether free or united.
Crenate Of leaf margins with rounded teeth.
Deciduous Trees which shed all leaves in autumn.
Dicotyledons Large group of flowering plants, with 2-lobed seedlings; usually net-veined leaves; flower parts usually 2, 4, 5 or multiples thereof.
Dioecious Male and female flowers on separate plants.
Ephemeral Short-lived; usually of sepals or petals.
Evergreen Plants with leaves persistent throughout the year.
Fibrous Thin and thread-like, as of some roots.
Filament The stalk of the stamen which carries the anther.
Floret A small flower, one of a dense cluster as in the family Compositae.
Frond Green leaf-like part of a fern.
Garigue Mediterranean vegetation characterised by low shrubs less than 1m tall on dry areas, often between the coast and the maquis.
Glabrous Smooth, without hairs.
Gland Organ of secretion, often on tip of hairs.
Glaucous Covered with bloom, bluish.
Halophyte A plant adapted to live in salty soil or water.
Herbaceous Not woody.
Heterostylous Having styles of varying lengths, e.g. some Primulas.
Hygroscopic Sensitive to moisture changes in the air.
Imbricate Closely overlapping at the edges, e.g. petals, leaves.
Inflorescence The complete flowering section of a stem; a collection of individual flowers together, e.g. Daisy, Orchid, Foxglove.
Involucre A collar of bracts beneath a flower head, e.g. in Compositae.
Labellum Lip; a modified petal, or fused petals, distinct from other petals, especially in Orchids and the Labiatae and Scrophulariaceae.
Maquis Thickets of shrubs, 2m or more tall, often dense, with scattered trees; characteristic of the Mediterranean region.
Monocotyledons A large group of flowering plants with a 1-lobed seedling, usually parallel-veined leaves, flower-parts usually 3 or 6.

Monoecious With unisexual flowers, both on same plant.
Moraine Stony debris deposited by glaciers.
Nectar Sweet substance produced by plants to attract insects.
Node A point on the stem where one or more leaves arise.
Obovate Egg-shaped, broadest at the top.
Ovate Egg-shaped, broadest at the base.
Ovary The lowest part of the pistil, enclosing ovules.
Ovule Small egg-like structure, which develops into a seed after fertilisation.
Palmate Divided in a hand-like way, usually of leaves.
Panicle A type of inflorescence branched and spreading, e.g. Sea-Kale and some Grasses.
Parasite A plant completely dependent upon other plants for its nutriment.
Perennial A plant which lives for more than 2 years, usually flowering each year.
Perfect Of a flower; possessing both stamens and pistil.
Perianth Floral leaves as a whole, whether distinct sepals and petals, e.g. Buttercup, or all similar and coloured, e.g. Lilies.
Petal One of the inner ring of floral leaves, usually large and coloured.
Pinnate The arrangement of leaflets in 2 rows.
Pistil The flower's female reproductive organ composed of stigma, style and ovary.
Pollen Small grains which contain the male reproductive cells.
Pollination The transference of pollen from the stamens to a stigma; in cross-pollination, to the stigma of a different flower.
Pollinia A structure formed from a mass of pollen grains in Orchid flowers.
Raceme Long inflorescence with stalked flowers.
Radical Of leaves growing directly from the stem base or rhizome.
Reticulate Strongly net-veined.
Revolute Rolled downwards or on to the underside (of leaves).
Rhizome Perennial underground stem.
Saprophyte A plant completely dependent upon dead organic matter for its nutriment.
Sepal One of the outer ring of floral leaves, typically green but not always.
Sessile Without a stalk.
Sheath The base of a leaf enveloping the stem.
Sinuate Having a wavy margin.
Spathulate Of leaves; spoon-shaped, like a spatula.
Spike Long inflorescence with sessile flowers.
Spikelet One or more florets in a group; of grass flowers.
Spur Hollow tubular extension of a flower often containing nectar.
Stamen One of the male reproductive organs of a flower.
Staminode An infertile stamen, often reduced in size.
Stigma The receptive surface of the pistil to which pollen adheres.
Stipule A small leaf-like growth at the base of the leaf stalk.
Stolon A creeping stem, usually above ground, which roots and produces new plants.
Striate Striped with long narrow depressions or ridges.
Style The stalk-like connection between the ovary and stigma.
Subtend The way in which a bract or leaf encloses a flower between itself and the stem.
Tap root A solid descending main root.
Taxonomy The classification of plants and animals in systematic order.
Tendril A thin curled sensitive climbing organ.
Terrestrial Plants growing in the ground, i.e. most European flowering plants.
Transpiration Loss of water vapour through leaf pores.
Trifoliate A leaf with 3 leaflets.
Tuber A swollen part of the stem or root, formed annually and usually underground; stores food.
Umbel An inflorescence in which the flower stalks arise together from the top of the main stem, like an umbrella.
Unilateral One-sided.
Xerophyte A plant adapted for very dry conditions, e.g. deserts, sand dunes.

Index of English Names

Page numbers refer to descriptive text;
photographs are on the same page or facing page.

Index of Latin Names

Page numbers refer to descriptive text;
photographs are on the same page or the facing page.